American
Indian
Moses

by

Timothy Dom Bucci

Second Edition edited by Mark Steven Kovacic and
Christos George Frentzos, the author's grandsons, with the
author's approval of all substantive changes.

Third Edition edited by the author's grandsons (George A.
Kovacic, Mark S. Kovacic, and Christos G. Frentzos) with
special assistance from Joseph Catone, Jr.

ISBN 978-0-9724860-0-2

Cover Art Work – Kelly Kovacic

Contents

Acknowledgments

I would like to dedicate this book to my wife of 68 years, Mary; to my two daughters, Mrs. Phyllis Bucci Kovacic and Mrs. Marlea Bucci Frentzos; and to my six grandchildren. My prayer is that this book and the **Bible** and **Translated Ancient Nephite Records** will be their guiding light and salvation through Jesus Christ our Lord.

I wish to inform the readers that I am not affiliated with any of the latter-day church factions (commonly referred to as Mormons). However, I am associated with an independent church group that comes out of the same restoration movement. I believe the **Bible** and the **Translated Ancient Nephite Records** (the *Book of Mormon*) to be the word of God.

Some of the personal opinions expressed in this book are my own and are not those of The Church of Jesus Christ (with world headquarters in Monongahela, Pennsylvania) of which I am a Minister.

Timothy Dom Bucci
1975

About The Author

Timothy Dominic Bucci was born in Monongahela, Pennsylvania in 1909. He attended high school and graduated from Hall's Business College in Youngstown, Ohio. Mr. Bucci was ordained a Minister in January 1943 and was subsequently ordained to the office of Evangelist in September 1950.

The author has performed missionary work throughout the United States and has spoken extensively to Native Americans in Oklahoma. Mr. Bucci has also spoken to Native Americans on reservations in the state of New York, such as the Seneca, Cattaraugus, Allegheny and Tuscarora. He visited the San Carlos and White River Reservation in Arizona and the Cherokee Reservation in North Carolina. Mr. Bucci was also personally acquainted with the late Chief Clinton Rickard of the Tuscarora Nation.

From 1945 to 1950, Mr. Bucci was the Pastor of the Girard, Ohio Mission and he served as Pastor of the Youngstown, Ohio Branch for various periods until 1986. After residing in Youngstown, Ohio from 1916 to 1986, Mr. Bucci moved to Erie, Pennsylvania with his wife, Mary

Mr. Bucci has authored several booklets, including, *Apostasy & Restoration* and *Jew & American Indian,* and the book *Jesus Christ the Messiah* and has had various articles published in newspapers and in a religious periodical called the *Gospel News.* He has also appeared on various television announcements and a television talk show during the late 1970's and early 1980's.

Preface

In 1975 a small but mighty book was published. There were only several hundred copies printed at that time. Those close to the author of the book held on tightly to their copies since it was out of print before it could gain the audience it deserved. The book I am referring to is "American Indian Moses."

We will backtrack for a moment to the late 1950's; would-be-author Timothy Dom Bucci is speaking to me of the great promises in God's plan for the Native Peoples of the Americas. I distinctly remember him talking at great length concerning the divine origin of the *Translated Ancient American Writings* commonly known as the *Book of Mormon.* As I grew older his encouraging words and the example he set in his life as a disciple of Jesus Christ left a great impression on me.

The culmination of his life dedicated to such a beautiful cause was brought forth in the initial printing of this book. Timothy D. Bucci's calling as a messenger, to spread the news of the brilliant future of the indigenous peoples of the Americas, was brought to paper and ink in the form of "American Indian Moses." Almost thirty years after the first printing a newly updated version is now available to all lovers of truth who desire to understand one of God's great unalterable truths.

Never in the history of the United States of America has there been a greater need for a concise composition concerning the future events, which we will be swept up into. Never has there been a greater need for the light of Truth to dispel the spiritual heavy darkness that surrounds both the Native American and the citizens of this nation. I have waited with great enthusiasm for the opportunity to share the information in this book with those who I believe will not only find merit in it, but comfort and hope as it looks to the great events of the near future for both American Indians and Israel. And if not at first then maybe through the workings of the Great Spirit its truth will be confirmed.

Read this book thoughtfully and prayerfully because its topic is timely and relevant to each and every one of us and most importantly to the Native Peoples of North, Central and South America.

George A. Kovacic, Eldest Grandson
Miami, Florida, December 2002

Preface to the 2017 Edition

The first two editions of this work included an addendum regarding the Middle East and future events. Many of those events transpired, such as the capture of Saddam Hussein of Iraq. The family felt that the addendum needed to be updated, particularly showing the similarities between the *State of Israel* and Native Americans. To accomplish this goal, we used our grandfather's writings, including the title of a pamphlet, *Jew and American Indian,* which he first published in the late 1950s. See Chapters 17 and 18.

To the reader: Scriptural references were not included to make the book easier to read. To those who would like to verify the quoted scripture or delve deeper, feel free to use your scriptural concordances or your favorite electronic search engine. Such a search engine is available at the following sites: www.TheChurchofJesusChrist.org; www.First-Voices.org; or go to Google Play and search "Bible and Book of Mormon" from The Church of Jesus Christ, headquartered in Monongahela, PA.

Introduction

In this book I will endeavor to convey the great things God has in store for the **American Indians** (or **Native Americans**) in the near future. The fact is that American Indians of the present United States were nearly annihilated by our governments and early European settlers, and a remnant was driven from their homelands and placed on reservations. There they suffered dire poverty, hunger, lack of economic opportunity and social acceptance, and poor health and education. Since 1900, the Indian population has more than tripled. The American Indians in Mexico, Central America, and South America, who likewise suffered greatly, number into the millions.

Some writers and historians consider our handling of this, our first minority problem, a disgrace. This pattern held for four centuries, from the day of the first European settlements until well into the twentieth century.

The Ancient Israelites, who were in bondage and slavery for about 400 years and under severe oppression, hard labor, and untold sufferings in ancient Egypt, were sent a *Deliverer* from God (Moses) who by the power of God, performed many signs, miracles, and wonders, and led the Israelites out of Egypt. Similarly, God is going to send a *Deliverer* or *American Indian Moses* in the near future to lead the American Indians out of their terrible situation.

This *American Indian Moses* is going to be highly esteemed among his people. God will give him a commandment to do a work for them, which will be of great worth in bringing them to the knowledge of His covenants. He will do no other work but what the LORD commands him and he will be great in the eyes of the LORD. He will be great like Moses.

The *American Indian Moses* will receive power from the LORD to bring forth God's word and knowledge of the American Indians' origin and of Jesus Christ, who once walked the Americas, as well as the true points of Jesus' doctrine. He will bring deliverance, unity, and salvation to the American Indian.

The material used in this book is taken from history books, the Bible and Translated Ancient Nephite Record. This latter record was revealed by a messenger of God to Joseph Smith, Jr. in 1823. It was buried in a hill not far from his home near Palmyra, New York, in the village of Manchester.

After being given permission to take the record by the messenger of God, he was given the gift and the power of God to translate it the English language from its original *Reformed Egyptian language.* The result is a book given to the world in 1830 and is commonly known as the *Book of Mormon,* although I will often refer to it as the Translated Ancient Nephite Record (as will be explained in the upcoming chapters).

This record contains a history of the forefathers of the American Indian, their origin and destiny, as well as many prophecies concerning their restoration. It contains a secular and sacred history of two great ancient American civilizations. This record has been rashly judged and misrepresented by many people. By some, it has been represented as a work of fiction, by others a new Bible, and by others the most ingenious literary work ever put together. Much has been published against the *Book of Mormon* and most of it by those who had never seen the book, or those who read it with a biased mind, to find fault. Let me urge you to read the book for yourself. There is an adage, which goes, "Judge not a book by its cover." The Apostle Paul said, "Prove all things, and hold fast to that which is good." (1 Thessalonians 5:21)

Chapter One

The Ancient Israelites

In order to convey the great things that are in store for the American Indians we must go into the history of the ancient Israelites. We believe that most Native Americans are direct descendants from the ancient Israelites (often referred to as the *House of Israel*), and in particular from two Israelite families who migrated from Jerusalem (around 600 BC) to America landing on the western coast of Central or South America (around 592 BC). We will go into detail later in the book concerning their actual migration and the dealings they had with God. Due to this lineage, the prophecies in the Bible concerning the restoration of the House of Israel apply to the American Indian as well.

Modern day Israelites (or Jews) can trace their origin back forty centuries to a man called Abraham. He was born and lived in a place called Ur of the Chaldees (1967 BC). Abraham's former name was Abram. God changed it to Abraham, which means *Father of a Multitude*. His complete faith and obedience in God caused him to be called the *Friend of God*. He lived in a day when people lived in spiritual transgression and idolatry. God selected this man to reestablish for himself a holy, righteous and peculiar people.

Now the Lord said unto Abram get you out of your country, and from your kindred, and from your father's house, unto a land that I will show you: And I will make of you a great nation, and I will bless you, and make your name great; and you will be a blessing: And I will bless them that bless you, and curse him that curses you: And in you shall all families of the earth be blessed.

This is the first covenant God made with Abraham. The latter part of this covenant clearly indicates the coming of a Savior through his posterity whereby all of the families of the earth would be blessed. God made other covenants with Abraham and to his son Isaac and grandson Jacob (it was through Jacob's descendants that the covenants would be fulfilled).

1

Jacob had a twin brother, Esau. Because Jacob and his mother deceived their father and acquired the family blessing that belonged to Esau, Jacob feared Esau.

Many years after Jacob had fled from his parents and brother (Esau had threatened to kill him) Jacob made his way back to his brother's home. On the way he came to a brook where he prayed earnestly to the Lord for help. He then gathered his family and sent them ahead, crossing the brook, but he remained alone on the other side of it to continue praying to God.

While he was alone, a strange person took hold of him and wrestled with him all night. This strange person was a messenger from God. They wrestled so hard that Jacob's thigh was put out of joint in the struggle. And the messenger of God said, "Let me go, for the day breaks," and then added, "Your name shall no more be called Jacob, but Israel, that is, he who wrestled with God. For you have wrestled with God and have won the victory." Thus was the name of Jacob changed to **Israel**.

Israel had twelve sons and eventually, after many generations, they were called the *Twelve Tribes of Israel, the Children of Israel, or Israelites.* Israel's last two sons were **Joseph** and Benjamin, from his wife Rachel, whom he loved dearly.

Now Israel loved Joseph more than all his children, because he was the son of his old age and the first son of his wife Rachel. Jacob made Joseph a coat of many colors, indicating that he was his favorite. When his brothers saw this they hated him. Joseph had the gift of spiritual dream and had several dreams from the Lord, which revealed that he would someday become very prominent and his brothers would pay homage to him. This made the brothers hate and envy him all the more.

One day, when Joseph was about seventeen years of age, he went out into the field where his brothers were feeding the flocks. When they saw him coming they conspired to slay him, so they first cast him into a deep pit. However, one of his brothers, Judah, had compassion for him and said, "Let us not kill him, but sell him to the Ishmaelites" who were on their way to Egypt. (Ishmaelites were distance relatives of the Israelites and were traders). Thus Joseph became a servant in Egypt, but not for long, for the Lord was with him.

Meanwhile, Joseph's brothers had taken his coat of colors and dipped it in the blood of a goat and presented it to their father, Israel, and said, "This we have found." Israel's heart was broken for he thought that a wild beast devoured his son, and he mourned for many days, weeping for the loss of his son.

While in Egypt, Joseph was a servant to a powerful man, but was falsely accused of a crime he did not commit. He spent time in prison, but even there he rose to be the administrator for the warden. Because Joseph had the spirit of the Lord, he interpreted several dreams for other prisoners and eventually for Pharaoh, King of Egypt. By interpreting Pharaoh's dream correctly (when none else could), he saved the Egyptians from starvation when a great famine hit the land of Egypt and the lands around it. Due to his abilities as an interpreter of dreams and an able administrator, Pharaoh promoted Joseph to the position of second-in-command in all of Egypt.

Joseph married Asenath, the daughter of Potipherah, priest of On, an Egyptian. He had two sons, the name of the first-born was Manasseh, meaning "one who causes to forget" and that of the second was Ephraim, meaning "restored." Most **American Indians** are descendants of Joseph and his two sons, thus at times in this book, the term *Seed of Joseph* or *fruit of Joseph's loins* will be used to refer to the American Indians.

Because the famine in Egypt reached all of the lands around it, Joseph's brothers eventually came to Egypt to buy grain. After several meetings, Joseph revealed himself to them and had them bring their families and his father to Egypt to live.

Israel was advanced in age and realized he would not live much longer, so he called his sons together and blessed each of them. The greatest blessings fell upon Judah (the Jews and from whence Jesus Christ came) and Joseph. Joseph then brought his two sons, Manasseh and Ephraim, to his father so that he may bless them. And great was the blessing that Israel pronounced upon the two sons of Joseph: a blessing that someday their posterity would migrate to a land, a choice land above all other lands, and they would become a great nation. This choice land given by Israel to his grandsons, as I will show, refers to the Western Hemisphere (North, Central and South America).

Chapter Two

Moses, The Lord's Deliverer

Joseph died at the age of one hundred and ten and was embalmed and put in a coffin in Egypt. There he remained for several hundred years. He requested that when the Israelites were delivered from bondage, they would take his body with them.

After many generations and being in bondage for about four hundred years and under severe sufferings, hard labor, oppression, and slavery for about two and a one-half centuries, God sent them a *Deliverer,* the man we commonly call **Moses**.

Many years after Joseph, there came a new King who had not known him. This new Pharaoh realized that the children of Israel were multiplying quickly. He told his court, "Behold the children of Israel are more and mightier. Come, let us deal wisely with them lest they multiply." So he afflicted them and made their lives bitter and burdensome, but the more the Egyptians afflicted them, the more they multiplied. The Israelites were also called *Hebrews* and the king commanded the midwives to destroy the male Hebrews and save the females. However, the midwives feared God and failed to do that, so he commanded the people to cast all male children into the river.

At this time there was a man and his wife who were from the tribe of Levi, having a son called Aaron and a daughter Miriam. The wife gave birth to a second son. She hid him for about three months, and when she could no longer hide him, she made an ark of bulrushes and daubed it with slime and with pitch and put the child in it; then she placed it among the rushes in the river. His sister, Miriam, stood afar off to see what would be done with the child.

The daughter of Pharaoh and her maidens came down to the river to wash. When she saw the ark, she told one of her maidens to fetch it. When she opened it and saw the child, the babe wept. She had compassion on him and said, "This is one of the Hebrews' children." Miriam, the sister of the child, approached the King's daughter and said, "Shall I go and call you a nurse of the Hebrew women." The princess agreed and the child went and brought the baby's mother. She nursed the child and after he grew, brought him to the princess becoming her son. The princess called the baby **Moses** because he was drawn from the water. Moses, being raised by his own mother, no doubt learned something about the Hebrews and his people, the Israelites, and perhaps also, the knowledge of the true living God.

Moses lived in the King's palace as the son of Pharaoh's daughter, learning the ways of the Egyptians. When he was forty years old he went out among his brethren and saw their burdens. When he saw an Egyptian beating a Hebrew he murdered the Egyptian and hid the body in the sand. And when he went out the second day, two men of the Hebrews were arguing and Moses said to him that did wrong, "Why do you smite your fellow?" And the man responded, "Who made you a prince and a judge over us? Do you intend to kill me, as you did the Egyptian?" And Moses feared, and said, "Surely this thing is known." When Pharaoh heard about the incidents he sought to slay Moses, but Moses fled from Pharaoh's palace and dwelt in the land of Midian.

By faith Moses refused to be called the son of Pharaoh's daughter, choosing rather to suffer affliction with the people of God than to enjoy the pleasures of sin for a season. He lived in the land of Midian and there he married Zipporah, the daughter of Jethro. She bore him two sons.

In time, the king of Egypt died, and the Israelites cried unto the Lord because of their enslavement and bondage. God heard their cries and remembered his covenant with Abraham, Isaac, and Jacob.

At this time, Moses had lived in the land of Midian for forty years, so he was now eighty years old. Being a shepherd all these years, he led a flock to the backside of the desert, and came to the mountain of God, Mount Horeb. And the Angel of the Lord appeared to him in a flame of fire out of the midst of a bush: and he looked, and behold, the bush burned with fire, but was not consumed.

Moses said, "I will turn aside, and see this great sight, why the bush is not burnt." And when the Lord saw that he turned aside to see, God called unto him out of the midst of the bush, and said, "Moses, Moses." And he answered, "Here am I." And the Lord said, "Do not get close, but first take your shoes from off your feet, for the place where you stand is holy ground. I AM the God of your father, the God of Abraham, Isaac, and Jacob." And Moses hid his face; for he was afraid to look upon God.

And the Lord then spoke to Moses and said:

> I have seen the affliction of my people who are in Egypt, and have heard their cry by reason of their taskmasters; for I know their sorrows. I am come down to deliver them out of the hand of the Egyptians, and to bring them up out of that land unto a good land and a large land flowing with milk and honey. I have heard their cry and have seen the oppression wherewith the Egyptians oppress them. I will send you unto Pharaoh that you may bring my people, the children of Israel, out of Egypt.

Moses responded to God, "Who am I, that I should go unto Pharaoh, and that I should bring forth the children of Israel out of Egypt." And the Lord said, "Certainly I will be with you." Then Moses said, "When I come to the children of Israel and say to them, 'The God of your fathers has sent me unto you,' and they shall say unto me, 'What is his name?' what shall I say unto them?" And God said, "**I AM THAT I AM** and say unto them **I AM** has sent me unto you."

This wondrous miracle that Moses witnessed in the desert, the bush that burned without being consumed, marked his beginning as the "Deliverer" of the Israelites in Egypt. The Lord said through Moses concerning the Israelites, "I will bring you out from under the burdens of the Egyptians and I will redeem you and I will take you to me for a people, and I will be to you a God. I have surely seen the afflictions of my people, which are in Egypt." God says to Pharaoh: "Let my people go."

As a side note, I would like to point out that the Lord had chosen the Israelites for a peculiar destiny as His Holy People, through whom all the families of the earth would be blessed. They were not chosen because of their great number or their powerful armies, but because he wanted a righteous people. The Christians as well as the Jews have this understanding.

The *unconsumed* burning bush is a *type and a shadow* (that is, a symbol of something to come) of the Israelites or their remnants going through the fires of oppression and persecution, and yet were miraculously preserved down through the centuries to this present day. Just before and during World War Two, approximately six million Jews were killed by Nazi Germany. The Jews' scattering and subsequent sufferings were due to their eventual disobedience and failure of accepting Jesus of Nazareth as the Messiah. Subsequently, they were scattered throughout the world. However, God has not forsaken them and the covenants that God made with Abraham, Isaac, and Jacob (Israel) and declared by the prophets that someday (in the near future) they will be restored to the land of their inheritance. I will provide more information about that restoration in later chapters, but it is interesting to note that since the coming forth of the Translated Ancient Nephite Record and the establishment of the State of Israel in the land of Palestine in 1948, God has set forth His hand the second time in fulfilling His promise in bringing about the restoration of the House of Israel.

When God called Moses to return to Egypt to lead the Hebrews or Israelites out of Egypt, Moses became frightened, not only of the Egyptians, but also of his ability to convince the Israelites that God sent him. Moses said, "They will not believe me, nor hearken to my voice." And the Lord said unto him. "What is that in your hand?" And he said, "A rod." "Cast it on the ground," said the Lord; Moses did and it became a serpent. "Now put forth your hand and take it by the tail." He put forth his hand and grabbed it so it became a rod. The Lord now told him, "Put your hand in your bosom" and he did. "Take it out." And when he complied, his hand was leprous as snow. The Lord again told him, "Put your hand in your bosom and take it out," and when he did his hand was restored to normal as the other flesh. This gave Moses courage; still he complained that he was unable to speak before the King and the Israelites, because he was slow of speech and tongue. And the Lord told him that he would be with him and teach him what to say. He added that Moses' brother Aaron was an eloquent speaker and Aaron would accompany Moses.

With the Lord with him, Moses made preparation to go to Egypt to stand before Pharaoh and the Elders of the Hebrew children. However, he was confronted with great opposition. When he arrived in Egypt, he called for all the Elders of the Israelites and related unto them all that God had told him and that he had come to deliver them from bondage. Moses and

Aaron went before Pharaoh and informed him that he came to lead the Israelites out of Egypt. Moses said to him, "Thus saith the Lord God of Israel, **LET MY PEOPLE GO**." Pharaoh's heart became hardened and he refused to let them go.

Because the Lord was with Moses and Aaron, they began to demonstrate the power of God before Pharaoh. The Lord warned Moses that Pharaoh would request a miracle. He told him to have Aaron cast down the rod and it would become a serpent. And so it happened; Aaron threw down the rod and it became a serpent, according to the word of the Lord. Pharaoh called his wise men, sorcerers, and magicians, and they also performed the same miracle. However, the serpent of Moses and Aaron swallowed up the serpents of the Egyptians. This episode clearly indicates that although evil is powerful and can perform miracles, God's power is greater and above all. Despite the display of God's power, Pharaoh refused to let the Israelites go.

The Lord said to Moses, "Go to the King in the morning and have Aaron your brother strike the river with the rod and all waters shall turn to blood. All living fishes shall die and the waters shall stink and be undrinkable." Moses and Aaron did as the Lord commanded and so it was done. Yet Pharaoh's heart was hardened and he would not let the Israelites go. This was the first of the so-called *plagues,* (a wide spread affliction, calamity or pestilence). During this plague and the ones that followed, the Israelites lived in a place called Goshen in northern Egypt and none of these plagues came upon them.

The following is a brief account of the plagues that subsequently came upon Egypt. Aaron stretched forth his rod again and the whole land of Egypt was covered with frogs. Still Pharaoh would not let the Israelites go. After the frogs, Aaron smote the dust of the earth again and lice covered the ground, upon man and beast. When the wise men and magicians of Pharaoh saw this they said to him, "This is the finger of God." The next plague was swarms of flies. They were in the house of Pharaoh, his servants, and in all the houses of the Egyptians. Pharaoh began to weaken and said to Moses and Aaron to take his people, worship God, but do not go very far. Moses would call upon God to remove these plagues and the Lord would hear and remove them. After the plagues were taken away, Pharaoh would break his promise.

More plagues came, including: Murrain (that is, a disease such as anthrax, foot-and-mouth, or tick fever) upon the cattle, horses, asses, camels, oxen, and sheep; then boils upon the Egyptians; then hail in all the land; and finally, darkness for three days. Again, I want to remind you that during all these plagues, the Israelites in the land of Goshen experienced none of them. The Lord protected them. The Lord said to Moses, "I will bring one more plague upon Pharaoh and Egypt and afterwards he will let you and your people go." This last plague involved the **Passover**. The Hebrew name for Passover is "Pesach." It was the tenth plague. The institution of the Passover was in the following manner. First, the Lord spoke to Moses, saying,

> Speak to all the congregation of Israel that on the tenth day of this month they shall take to them every man a lamb, according to the house of their fathers, a lamb for a house. Your lamb shall be without blemish, a male of the first year. Take it from the sheep or goats and on the fourteenth of the month the congregation of Israel shall kill it in the evening. They shall take of the blood, and strike it on the two side posts and on the upper doorposts of the houses.

> And they shall eat the flesh that night, roasted with fire, and thus shall ye eat with your loins girded, your shoes on your feet, and your staff in your hand; and ye shall eat it in haste: it is the Lord's Passover. I will pass through the land of Egypt this night, and will smite all the first-born in the land of Egypt. I will execute judgment: I am the Lord.

> And the blood shall be to you a token upon the houses where you are: and when I see the blood, I will pass over you, and the plague shall not be upon you, when I smite the land of Egypt. And let this day be unto you for a memorial.

And it came to pass that at midnight, the Lord smote all the first-born in the land of Egypt, from the first-born of Pharaoh that sat on his throne unto the first-born of the captive that was in the dungeon, all of Pharaoh's servants, all of the Egyptians and even all the first-born of the cattle, so that there was a great cry in Egypt. For there was not a house where there was not one dead. The King called for Moses and Aaron and said, "Rise up, and get you forth from among my people, both ye and the children of Israel; and go, serve the Lord as ye have said." So finally Pharaoh let them go, only to regret it later. The children of Israel took their journey with Moses their leader and deliverer after being in bondage and slavery for many years.

The Passover was *a type and a shadow* of the coming of Jesus Christ. The Apostle Paul, wrote to the Corinthians of Greece over fourteen hundred years later that, "For even Christ our Passover is sacrificed for us." John the Baptist, in the days of Jesus, said, "Behold the lamb of God, which takes away the sin of the world." Jesus made preparations for the celebration of the Passover with his twelve Apostles and it was the **last supper** before his crucifixion.

After about four hundred and thirty years in Egypt, the Israelites went out in great haste taking their own possessions and whatever items the Egyptians gave them. Their bread dough in pans that had not risen is called the *unleavened bread.* The Jewish name for the unleavened bread is *matzos.* The Jews to this present day hold the Passover supper once a year as a memorial of how God freed them from the bondage of the Egyptians.

When the great host of Israelites left Egypt, the Lord God miraculously provided for them a pillar of cloud by day and a pillar of fire by night to lead them on their way. And Moses took the bones of Joseph with them, as he requested before his death. We will continue the saga of Moses and the Israelites in the next chapter.

In closing this chapter, I would like to comment on the above events. God raised kings, judges, and leaders for the Israelites down through the centuries. God called Moses to be a great leader and Deliverer, so shall it be in these last days when God will call another Israelite to be a great leader and Deliverer. Later in the book, I will show that the American Indians are from the House of Israel and that they will have their own Deliverer (also called the Choice Seer). I call him the American Indian Moses, for he will be like Moses possessing the same great power of God in bringing about the restoration of the House of Israel, especially the American Indian in this Western Hemisphere. Being a remnant of the House of Israel, therefore, American Indians are included in the promises and covenants God made with the Jews and the tribes of Israel. He will restore to the Jews the land given to Abraham and to the American Indian the land of America.[1]

Chapter Three

Out of Egypt & Into the Wilderness

Pharaoh and his servants deeply regretted letting the Israelites go. He took six hundred chosen chariots, and all the chariots of Egypt, and captains over every one of them. His horsemen and his army went out in pursuit of the Israelites, and he intended to bring them back or to destroy them. When the Israelites learned that the Egyptian army was not far behind, they became frightened and said to Moses, "Why didn't you leave us alone, it would have been better to serve the Egyptians than to die in the wilderness." And Moses said to the people, "Fear ye not, stand still, and see the salvation of the Lord, which he will show you today, you shall see them again no more forever." At this time, the Israelites were facing the Red Sea. And the Lord told Moses, "Lift up your rod and stretch out your hand over the sea, and divide, and the children of Israel shall go on dry ground through the midst of the sea." Moses complied and stretched out his hand over the sea; and the Lord caused the sea to go back by a strong east wind all that night, and made the sea dry land, and the waters were divided.

The children of Israel went into the midst of the sea upon dry ground; and the waters were a wall to them on their right and left hands. The Egyptians pursuing, went in after them, even all Pharaoh's horses, his chariots, and his horsemen. The Egyptians said, "Let us flee, for the Lord fights for them." Then the Lord said to Moses, "Stretch your hand over the sea," and when he did, the waters returned to their strength and resumed their course. Now Pharaoh's horsemen and his army that went into the sea were drowned. There remained not so much as one of them. Thus the Lord saved Israel that day out of the hand of the Egyptians; and they saw the great work of the Lord, believed the Lord, and his servant Moses.

However, it wasn't long that the Israelites began to murmur against Moses and his brother Aaron in the wilderness, because of the lack of food and the hardship of traveling in the wilderness. Moses called upon God for help and the Lord said, "I will send you bread from heaven." And when the Israelites saw it on the ground the next morning they said, "What is it?" In Hebrew the word is **"manhu"** and from this came the name *manna*. He also sent upon the ground quail for meat. They were commanded to gather enough for one day at a time. Some disobeyed and intended to save some; however, it decayed and the odor was bad. This was a lesson that they should trust the Lord for their daily bread. And because the children of Israel remained in the wilderness for forty years, they only ate manna. During this forty-year trek, even their shoes and clothing did not wear out, but remained the same.

Despite all that the Lord had done for the Israelites, delivering them from slavery and bondage and many signs and wonders in the wilderness demonstrating the power of God through Moses, they would murmur and find fault with Moses and Aaron, his brother. However, God's judgment would fall upon them, and then they would repent and return to God.

Chapter Four

The Ten Commandments

In the third month after the Israelites left Egypt they came to Mount Sinai, the same mountain where Moses saw the burning bush and heard the voice of God. And there they camped for many days. Moses went up into the mountain, and the Lord spoke to him, saying, "Thus you shall say to the children of Israel, 'You have seen what I did to the Egyptians, now if you will obey my voice and keep my covenant, then you shall be a peculiar treasure to me above all people, a kingdom of Priests and an holy nation.'" Moses related to them all that the Lord had told him. At times, God would come down in a thick cloud to speak to them.

The children of Israel were warned to neither climb the mountain nor advance beyond its borders and if anyone did, man or beast, they must be killed. On the third day, the mountain was covered by a cloud and smoke, and lightning flashed from it. There was the noise of thunder and the mountain trembled. And when the people heard the voice of the Lord from out of the mountain saying, "I am the Lord your God, which have brought thee out of the land of Egypt, out of the house of bondage" they were filled with fear.

The Lord continued to speak to them and gave what is known as the **Ten Commandments**, one of the greatest sets of laws ever given.

1. You shall have no other gods before me.
2. You shall not make to yourself any graven image, or any likeness of anything that is in heaven above, or that is in the earth beneath, or that is in the water under the earth: You shall not bow down yourself to them, or serve them: for I the Lord your God am a jealous God.
3. You shall not take the name of the Lord in vain; for the Lord will not hold him guiltless that takes his name in vain.
4. Remember the Sabbath day, to keep it holy.
5. Honor your father and your mother: that the days may be long upon the land, which the Lord your God gives you.
6. You shall not kill.
7. You shall not commit adultery.

8. You shall not steal.
9. You shall not bear false witness against your neighbor.
10. You shall not covet your neighbor's house, nor your neighbor's wife, manservant, maidservant, ox, ass, nor anything that is your neighbor's.

I would like to go over these Ten Commandments with some explanations. First, "You shall have no other gods before me." It is evident that God does not want us to have any other god. He is supreme and the ruler of the universe.

Second, "You shall not make to yourself any graven image." This statement means that we shouldn't worship anything drawn, such as pictures, or any object made with human hands, such as statues or idols of any likeness in the heavens, in the earth, or in the waters beneath the earth, or the human mind (ungodly philosophies). "You shall not bow down to them, nor serve them: for I the Lord your God am a jealous God." Remember the Golden Calf and God's judgment upon Israel. God hates idolatry (the worship of man-made objects).

Third, "You shall not take the name of the Lord in vain." How often we hear profanity, taking the name of God and Jesus Christ in vain. It is not only the careless and cavalier use of the words God, Lord or Jesus Christ, but also the vulgar use of similar words or derivatives of those words. The commandment said, "For the Lord will not hold him guiltless that takes His name in vain."

Fourth, "Remember the Sabbath day, to keep it holy." We read in the creation that God ended his work on the sixth day, and He rested on the seventh day, blessed it and sanctified it. However, He does not call it the Sabbath day. We do not read in the scriptures that Adam, Noah, Abraham, Isaac, Jacob, Joseph, or Moses - until he was eighty years old - ever kept the seventh day as the Sabbath day. It wasn't until God gave it to Moses in the mountain for the Israelites in the wilderness, and for their posterity. For 2,500 years before Moses, there was no Sabbath-keeping recorded, no law. Now it became a law for the children of Israel and to be observed by them and their posterity as long as Israel remained a nation. It was a sign that they were God's people.

Jesus of Nazareth, whose mother, Mary, was a virgin and Joseph, his foster father, were Jews of the house of David. The miraculous birth of Jesus made him the Jewish Messiah

14

and the Son of God for the Christians. Jesus in his Jewish upbringing observed the Sabbath day or the seventh day of the week for worship and as a holy day, as well as a day of rest. Jesus said He "came not to destroy the law, but to fulfill it." When God completed the creation on the sixth day, He said, "It is very good." So He rested on the seventh day, blessed and sanctified it. When Jesus completed His mission and was placed on the cross, as the scriptures declare, "Behold the Lamb of God, who takes away the sin of the world." Before He died, He said, "It is finished," thus fulfilling the law, and in place he established a new covenant, the law of Christ. However, the Lord sanctioned the commandments of civil and moral laws He had given to Moses.

The law of grace or the law of Christ superseded the old law, bringing salvation, as it is written, "For by grace are ye saved through faith." When the Lord himself established the Church of Jesus Christ, He commissioned the Apostles to go out and preach the gospel to every creature. "He that believes and is baptized shall be saved; but he that believes not shall be damned." The Apostles of Jesus Christ, being inspired, instituted the commemoration of the Master's resurrection on Sunday, the first day of the week, calling it the **Lord's Day**. The Christians eventually called it the Sabbath Day. This took place in the early years of the fourth century. Therefore, the *Lord's Day* is appropriate for Sunday, the first day of the week. "Are you under the law or under grace?" The Apostle Paul says, "For you are not under law, but under grace." So, remember the Lord's Day and keep it holy.

The fifth commandment given to Moses and later written upon tablets of stone is, "Honor your Father and your Mother: that thy days may be long upon the land, which the Lord your God gives you." This is the first commandment with a promise. The Apostle Paul said, "Children, obey your parents in the Lord: for this is right; honor your Father and Mother, that it may be well with you, and you may live long on the earth." He also said in his letter to Timothy, a fellow worker in the gospel, that in the latter days (our days) the young would be disobedient to parents, unthankful, unholy, without natural affection, etc. Observing the situation in the world today, we see the precise fulfillment of Paul's prediction. (I address these items in greater detail later in the book.)

This situation is not principally the fault of the young; in many cases the fault lies with the parents. Discipline begins in the home. Love for God and country should be displayed in the home as well. Parents should be an example to the children. The Apostle Paul also told parents not to stir their children up to anger.

The sixth commandment is, "You shall not kill." There is so much killing in the world today. In America, with the proliferation of weapons in the home and on the street, there are drive-by shootings, children ignorantly killing other children while playing with the weapons, murders committed during robberies, and even domestic disturbances ending in violent deaths.

There are also murders committed by drivers of automobiles who are under the influence of alcohol or illegal drugs. Finally, there are racially motivated murders and unnecessary military actions. In my conviction, I believe that this commandment is principally for premeditated murder or murder during the act of a crime. All of these things portray a complete disregard and disrespect for human life. There has been a tremendous controversy over the law of capital punishment; however, capital punishment is scriptural, given by the Lord to Moses and practiced in times past very crudely. Although it has returned in many states of the USA, its effectiveness as a deterrent to crime is still debated.

The seventh commandment is "You shall not commit adultery." This commandment is widely broken. It is the basic cause of the tremendous increase in divorce. It is running rampant in our high schools and colleges. Venereal disease is practically an epidemic in the United States, along with the newest sexually transmitted disease, acquired immune deficiency syndrome (AIDS). The offspring of the American people will be sick and diseased. God has condemned adultery, and caused his judgments to come upon the individual and nations collectively. Jesus said, "That whosoever looks on a woman to lust after her has committed adultery with her already in his heart." The punishment under the Law of Moses was stoning; a quick, albeit violent, means of deterring adultery.

The easy access to the filth that is being produced in our country is warping the minds of the people, especially the young. Pornography, obscene literature, and sex videos are contributing factors to crime and rape. Sex within marriage is blessed by God; marriage is a Godly institution. Outside marriage it is adultery (or fornication). Jesus said "But from the beginning of the creation, God made them male and female; for this cause shall a man leave his father and mother, and cleave to his wife; and the two shall be one flesh: so then they are no more two, but one flesh. What therefore God has joined together, let not man put asunder." This teaching, as well as several references in the Old and New Testaments, condemns homosexuality as a life-style choice. The Apostle Paul told the Romans that,

> For this cause God gave them up unto vile affections, for even their women did change the natural use into that which is against nature. And likewise also the men, leaving the natural use of the woman, burned in their lust one toward another; men with men working that which is unseemly, and receiving in themselves that recompense of their error which was meet.

The eighth commandment is "You shall not steal." The robbery and theft that goes on is appalling. Principally it is to obtain money or the possessions of others. The Apostle Paul puts it very plainly - money is not evil, it's a necessity, but it's the "love of money" (greed) that is evil and disruptive. And for the love of money, robbery and murder are committed. Today, "white-collar" crime is rampant. This term hides the true crime of stealing. Educated people and professionals (and even our elected representatives) are now stealing from their employers and from innocent people everywhere. Apostle Paul told the Saints in Ephesus, "Let him that stole steal no more: but rather let him labor, working with his hands the thing which is good, that he may have to give to him that needs."

The ninth commandment is "You shall not bear false witness against your neighbor." Basically, it is lying about something or someone; therefore, tell no lie, or you are breaking the ninth commandment. Today, few take this seriously. Lying has become habitual to many people. Even to the extent where we have sugar coated it by calling them "little, white lies." Even in courts of law people lie so we have a penalty for perjury.

The tenth and last commandment on the tablets of stone that were given to Moses is "You shall not covet." The word covet means a form of desire, and can be for good or evil. However, here in the Ten Commandments it is forbidden because it refers to a fleshly desire to possess what belongs to another person, a jealous desire, and a craving desire to satisfy the flesh.

These are the Ten Commandments given to Moses for the children of Israel; they are considered moral and civil laws. However, there were many more laws given by the Lord for the children of Israel, such as priestly, ceremonial, and dietary laws.

Chapter Five

Journey to Canaan and the Promised Land

Moses, the great deliverer, was instrumental in the hands of the Lord. He performed many signs and miracles and finally accomplished the task of releasing Israel from under the yoke of Egyptian bondage. Yet what confronted Moses on the other side of the Red Sea and in the wilderness was much harder. To marshal the Israelites into a community and a nation of people required the gifts of a general, judge, and legislator. The Israelites often murmured and were disobedient, and even rebellious at times, bringing the displeasure of God upon them.

After being in the wilderness for forty years, a wilderness they could have crossed in a few months, the Israelites came near the borders of the land of Canaan. Because of Moses' anger toward the Israelites in one instance, The Lord did not permit him to go into the land of Canaan (it was later called Palestine). At this time, Moses was one hundred and twenty years old. The final scene in the great leader and deliverer's life came when he received the summons to go up into Mount Nebo, and there, after viewing the land of promise in its entire length and breadth, he died. Yes, upon the heights of Pisgah, in the land of Moab, Moses died and the Lord buried him in a valley, over against Bethpeor. To this day no one knows where his grave is. The children of Israel wept for Moses for thirty days in the desert on the plains of Moab. There was never another prophet in Israel like Moses, of whom the Lord knew face to face.

But the children of Israel had to move on, so God called another man, who became the leader of the Israelites. His name was Joshua. Although he had been with the Israelites from the days of bondage in Egypt, it was now time for him to be used by God in an even greater extent. He led the Israelites into battle with the inhabitants of the land of Canaan and conquered many nations, until it became their land as God promised Abraham, Isaac, and Jacob. After the death of Joshua, the children of Israel would drift into sin and transgression, idolatry, and abominations, forgetting their God who had done so much for them. For these reasons, the Lord left them to suffer, and caused their enemies to become their masters. However, when they would remember the Lord, He would deliver them.

The Lord raised judges and kings to lead them; some of the kings were evil, some were not. Nevertheless, the people would often go into sin, influenced by either evil leaders or the pagan worshippers that surrounded their land. King Saul, King David, and King Solomon were men of great stature and were instrumental in the hands of God. Down through the centuries great prophets arose in the land of Palestine, warning the Israelites of their transgression and sin. The nation eventually divided into two countries, with separate capital cities. The northern kingdom consisted of ten of the tribes of Israel and the southern kingdom (under a king born of the house of David) consisted of the remaining two tribes (Judah and Benjamin). The tribe of Levi had become the priestly tribe and they were scattered throughout both kingdoms (by deducting them and then splitting the house of Joseph into two tribes representing Ephraim and Manasseh, the number of tribes remained at twelve). There was some mixing of the tribes over the years, as well.

Around 720 BC, the northern kingdom, with the city of Samaria as its capital, was taken captive by enemies (Assyrians) and dispersed throughout the North Country and possibly beyond. Later, around 589 BC, the southern kingdom, with the city of Jerusalem as its capital, was conquered and many of its inhabitants were carried captive into Babylon. They were allowed to return to Canaan and the city of Jerusalem about seventy-five years later. They remained in that geographic area until around 70 AD when the Romans destroyed Jerusalem and scattered the Jews around the known world.

For the ten tribes of the northern kingdom, it is not known who or where they are at the present time. However, in the Ancient Translated Nephite Record, we have learned that the **descendants of Joseph** (the Joseph who was sold by his brethren and carried to Egypt), are the **Native Americans or American Indians**. The **Jews** of today, who are mostly from the tribe of Judah, some from the tribe of Benjamin and some from the tribe of Levi, have been scattered or dispersed throughout the world for over 1900 years.

There are many prophecies in the Bible concerning the literal and physical restoration of the House of Israel. Many prophecies have been fulfilled in the past and many are being fulfilled today in bringing about the restoration of the House of Israel. The most confusing problem in the world today is the Middle East as evidenced by the recent wars in Afghanistan and Iraq, the Syrian civil war, and the continuing problems of terrorism in the region. Although America appears strong and capable, the continued degeneration of our morals, laws, and life-style, will surely bring the judgment of God down on us. The Ancient Translated Nephite Record says that Jesus Christ is the God of Americas and He must be worshipped and His commandments kept, or else God's judgment will be swift.

The prophecies concerning the **restoration** of the House of Israel include the Native Americans, for they are of the House of Israel. The Jews and the other tribes of Israel will be restored to the land of Palestine, their land of inheritance, and the Native Americans to America, their land of inheritance.

Therefore, in this book, I will endeavor to inform the reader of the origin of the Native American (Seed of Joseph) and the prophecies of a *Choice Seer* (who I call the **American Indian Moses**) who will come out of the Indian nation in the near future to lead his people to a new level of spirituality. He will be a powerful instrument in the hands of God as Moses was for the Children of Israel. But first let me discuss where the Native Americans came from and who their ancestors are.

Chapter Six

Origin of the American Indians

Ever since the discovery of the Western Hemisphere questions have been raised concerning the origin of the **Native American**. Theories abound concerning their origin, but nothing substantial or definite. Many writers have stated that the Indians are descendants of Mongolians who migrated over the ice land from Siberia to Alaska. Other writers have stated that there have been migrations from various parts of Asia, Polynesia, Malaysia, China, Japan, and Palestine. This may have occurred down through the centuries by individuals or small fishing parties or adventurers, all by accident or mistake. However, as I have stated, I will show that the American Indians are descendants of Joseph, who was sold by his brethren into the land of Egypt, migrating from Jerusalem, Palestine, about the year 600 BC. And I will show this, not by fanciful theory or irrelevant and misunderstood archeological findings, but by the revelation of God.

The material used to prove my point is taken from the Translated Ancient Nephite Record. It mostly deals with the migration of two Israelite families, the true forefathers of the majority of American Indians. It also details their dealings with God, as well as their spiritual and civil history. And just as important, it communicates their destiny and that of the land of America.

Before we go into the migration from Palestine, let me bring a point to your attention concerning the American Indians. You have often heard the terms "vanishing American" and the "forgotten American." While these could have been used near the end of the nineteenth century, they are no longer applicable. According to scholars, from the time of the discovery of the New World, about seven million Indians populated the U.S. and Canadian territories. In 1900 this number dramatically dropped to about 270,000.

But since 1900, the American Indian population has grown rapidly in the U.S. and is now back to almost three million.[2] In Mexico, Central America, and South America, the Indian population runs into the millions.

However the term *forgotten American* is still true. Indians have been driven from their land and placed on reservations, often in remote, desolate unproductive land, experiencing hunger, malnutrition, poverty, squalor, sickness, and discrimination, but not for long. Like the Israelites who suffered for about 400 years, until the Lord sent them a **Deliverer**, Moses, so shall the Lord send in the near future a *Choice Seer* or *Deliverer,* an *American Indian Moses,* who will come out of the Indian nation to deliver them after hundreds of years of sufferings, oppression, and discrimination.

The pre-Columbian Indians differed in their economic patterns, and were even more divided in political and language matters. Linguists count more than 500 distinct Indian languages within the United States and there were more tribes than dialects. Some tribes had considerable population and controlled large amounts of land. But the general Indian picture was one of hopeless division. This division made it easy for the Europeans to defeat the tribes one by one (even to have them fight against each other).

The Indian culture was admirable in many ways. Unfortunately, they were not as advanced militarily as the Europeans. The Indian was an experienced warrior and willing enough to fight, but he fought with the bow and arrow; the Europeans had horses, iron, and gunpowder. These items, plus the crusading spirit of the Europeans, helped them achieve victory. The struggle between the Gentiles (Europeans) and the American Indians (Israelite) was prophesied in the Translated Ancient Nephite Record.

> And it came to pass that I beheld many multitudes of the Gentiles upon the land of promise; and the wrath of God, that it was upon the seed of my brethren; and they were scattered before the Gentiles and were smitten.

The more advanced native peoples, the Aztecs of Mexico, the Incas of Peru, the Pueblos of the American Southwest, survived contact with the Europeans. When the Europeans came, these Indians were already living settled lives and were engaged in intensive agriculture under their native masters. After the conquest, they continued their farming pursuits, serving their new overlords much as they had their own chieftains. They blended their blood with that of the newcomers. Often they accepted Christianity (even if only in outward observances), and in time learned a bit about Old World culture from the Christian missionaries. Economic conflict was a central factor.

The Indians of the present United States relied heavily, although not entirely, on hunting and fishing. They therefore needed to reserve large wooded lands for these purposes. The Europeans, on the other hand, were primarily interested in farming. As they cleared the forests, they cut into tribal hunting grounds. The Indians then had a difficult choice -- they could depart or fight. Actually, they had no choice at all, for Indian wars ended in defeat and their removal to small tracts of lands set aside for them (reserves). Some Europeans tried to get along with the natives; however, they considered themselves superior to the Indians. The newcomers considered themselves and not the Indians as the discoverers of the New World. Furthermore, they insisted that the Indians adjust themselves to (or at least not interfere with) the intruders' economy.

Many Europeans and their descendants did not even attempt to be fair and if they could legally (and unethically) cheat the Indians out of their lands, so much the better. If not, the lands were taken anyway. Such arguments and attitudes explain why some writers and historians consider our handling of our first "minority problem" as disgraceful and shameful. Time after time, it was the same story -- early purchase of Indian lands, friction, and war, then removal of the tribes to the West or local reserves and reservations.

As the population of Indians declined, some people deplored their passing. Humanitarians formed Indian rights associations. Fair-minded authors praised the first Americans and criticized the Indian policy of the United States. The Indian problem, which has existed since the government decided more than a century ago that it was cheaper to buy off the Indian than kill him off, is still one of poverty, poor health, poor education, and lack of social acceptance, as well as lack of economic opportunity.

The Indians, as well as the newcomers, made many mistakes, bringing hardships and sufferings upon each other. The time is approaching when the American Indian will find his place here in the Americas. However, this will come about only when righteousness shall prevail. The wicked shall perish and the righteous spared. This gentile nation, who took this land, must also turn to righteousness or else they too shall be destroyed. Here is a prophecy taken out of the Translated Ancient Nephite Record.

> Cursed shall be the land [America] yea, this land, unto every nation, kindred, tongue, and people, unto destruction, which do wickedly, when they are fully ripe; and as I have said so shall it be; for this is the cursing and blessing of God upon the land [America] for the Lord cannot look upon sin with the least degree of allowance.

Another prophecy concerning America taken from the same record follows:

> Inasmuch as ye shall keep my commandments, ye shall prosper, and shall be led to a land of promise [America] yea, even a land which I have prepared for you; yea, a land which is choice above all other lands. For it is a choice land saith God, above all other lands, **wherefore I will have all men that dwell thereon that they shall worship me.**

Here is another prophecy from the same records in reference to this land, and the gentiles or non-Israelite/Americans that dwell on the land of promise (America).

> And now we can behold the decrees of God concerning this land, that it is a land of promise; and whatsoever nation shall possess it shall serve God, or they shall be swept off when the fullness of his wrath shall come upon them. And the fullness of his wrath cometh upon them when they are ripened in iniquity.

Americans, hear the word of the Lord and be obedient to His commandments!

Chapter Seven

Colonies to America

Before we explore the colonies that the Lord God led to America, let us go back about four hundred years before Abraham to the days of Noah. The Lord said, "My spirit shall not always strive with man." Prior to the great flood (deluge), God saw that the wickedness of men was great on the earth, and that every imagination of the thoughts of men's hearts was continually evil. It was so bad that God repented that he had created man, and it grieved Him in His heart. And the Lord said, "I will destroy man whom I have created from the face of the earth; both man, and beast, and the creeping thing, and the fowls of the air; for it repents me that I have made them." But the scriptures say that Noah found grace in the eyes of the Lord.

The earth was corrupt before God and filled with violence. (We have the same situation in the world today.) And God said to Noah, "The end of all flesh is come before me; for the earth is filled with violence through them; and, behold, I will destroy them with the earth. Make an Ark of gopher wood." Noah made the Ark according to the instructions of the Lord. At this time Noah was six hundred years old. His wife and his three sons and their wives were commanded to enter the Ark. Only eight people were saved from the great flood.

Along with Noah and his family, the Lord prepared all the animals of the earth so that they too could enter the Ark to be saved. Then came the rains, forty days and forty nights, until the waters covered the highest mountain. All living things perished except those in the Ark, and the waters remained upon the earth for one hundred and fifty days.

After the great flood and the waters receded from the face of the earth, the *Western Hemisphere* (the **Americas**) was isolated, and it was consecrated and blessed as an abiding place of a righteous and holy people. Colonies that came to America after the flood were warned by the prophets of God, saying, 'Inasmuch as you keep my commandments ye shall be blessed, and prosper in this land [America], and when not, you shall be judged, and destruction shall be your lot.' This prophecy was repeated three times and it has already been fulfilled twice.

According to archaeologists there flourished in America several great civilizations. In the Translated Ancient Nephite Record three migrations are depicted, and two great civilizations evolved. The first group migrated from the tower of Babel at the time of the confusion of tongues, about 2200 BC. They came by divine direction under the administration of two men who were brothers, one of them a spiritual seer. They, their families, and some of their friends composed the colony, traveled away from the Plains of Shinar (modern day Iraq), and crossed the ocean. They eventually landed on the coast of Central America.

This first colony brought records of the creation and fall of man and of the flood. Prophets arose among them with many predictions, including that of the promised Messiah and his redemption, as well as prophecies of what will occur in these modern times. They developed into a great, flourishing civilization, increasing in population rapidly, experiencing periods of spiritual unity, progress, and general advancement, as evidenced by archaeological discoveries. However, this civilization then declined and became weakened and divided by wickedness, contentions, and civil war. The result was that this first civilization became extinct about the time of the early development of the second colony, the first colony having destroyed itself and its entire population with the exception of one man. This last survivor lived about nine months with the third colony, which arrived around 589 BC.

The second colony left the city of Jerusalem in about 600 BC, preceding the destruction of that city and deportation of its inhabitants by Nebuchadnezzar, King of Babylon. A prophet of God and his son led this colony. Among the members of the colony were the prophet's sons and daughters, as well as a friend of his and his family. They were contemporary with the prophet Jeremiah, who warned the Jews of the pending destruction because of their wickedness and sin. This second colony was led by the arm of God, as manifested in the marvelous things He did for them. Crossing the Pacific Ocean, they landed on the western coast of the Americas. During the journey, these two families intermarried. They kept track of their lineage (family tree). Of particular interest is that they were descendants of Jacob's son Joseph, who was sold by his brethren. These Israelites of the second colony are the forefathers of many of the **American Indian**. Thus the term is sometimes used *the seed of Joseph.* Later in the book we shall go into greater detail regarding their migration to America, dealings with God, and the great prophecies recorded.

The third colony left Jerusalem about eleven years after the second colony, about 589 BC. This colony, composed of Israelites, included a young lad, who escaped the destruction of Jerusalem. He was the son of King Zedekiah of Judah. This colony landed in the vicinity of Central America. Sometime between 320 and 400 years later, they were discovered by the second colony. A portion of the second colony joined together with those of the third colony. However, they chose their kings from descendants of the second colony.

The second colony took with them from Jerusalem a set of records. These records included the five books of Moses and many of the books of the prophets, including the books of Isaiah and Jeremiah. Once in America, this colony kept the Law of Moses and its precepts and rituals with the understanding that they were to be observed until the coming of Christ. They truly worshipped God through their belief in Christ.

All three colonies were similar in that they were led by divine inspiration to a land declared to be a choice land above all other lands and that they were to become a righteous and holy people. This land was referred to as the land of promise.

After the arrival of the second colony to America, between 588 and 570 BC, contention arose among them. The two elder sons of the prophet became rebellious and unbelievers of the things of God. So the Lord caused a separation among the followers of the elder sons and those that believed in the things of God. He caused a skin of blackness to fall upon the unbelievers, thus they became a distinct people. There were times when they repented of their ways and believed in the things of God, and so the skin of blackness was removed.

Over the centuries, the two groups of the second colony intermingled. Eventually a separation occurred between those that believed in Christ and those that did not. This second separation continued until the believers were all destroyed. The remaining faction was cursed by God for their idolatry and sin. The descendants of this remaining group became known as **Native Americans** or **American Indians**. The day will come when they, as a people, will accept Christ and his pure gospel. When that occurs, their remaining curse will be removed and they shall become a white and delightsome people (believing in the God of Israel and His Son, Jesus Christ).

Now that I have introduced the colonies that came to America, the land of promise, a choice land above all other lands, let's move on to the specifics of their journeys and some of the more important events that occurred.

Chapter Eight

First Migration to America

As I previously explained, there were three migrations to America after the great flood. The first was about 2200 BC from the *Tower of Babel*. After the flood, the inhabitants of the earth had one language. As the people multiplied, they spread out toward the East and found a plain in the land of Shinar. And the people reasoned among themselves, "Let us build a city and a tower, whose top may reach to heaven; and let us make us a name, lest we be scattered abroad upon the face of the whole earth." The Lord saw the city and the tower that they were building. He said, "Behold, the people are one, and they have all one language; and this they are doing; and now nothing will be restrained from them that they imagine to do. Let us go down there and confound their language, that they may not understand one another's speech." Because the Lord confounded the language of all the inhabitants of the earth that place was called Babel. From there the Lord scattered them upon the face of the earth.

However, at this same time, there were two brothers, one of whom was large and mighty, a prophet and a seer with tremendous faith. The other brother, whose name was Jared, was also a man of faith, but of a different constitution. Jared asked his brother to cry to the Lord three times. The first time so that the Lord would not confound their language. The second time so that the Lord would not confound the language of their friends. And finally, the third time so that the Lord would lead them to a new land, choice above all other lands. Now the Lord not only heard each of the prayers, but he had compassion upon them and granted their requests.

The Lord said to the prophet after the third request:

Go and gather together your flocks, both male and female, of every kind; and also of the seed of the earth of every kind; and your family and friends, your brother and his family, and his friends and their families; go to a valley which is northward and there will I meet you I will go before you into a land that is choice above all the lands of the earth [America].

And there will I bless you and your seed, and raise up unto
me of your seed...a great nation.

The Lord came down in a cloud and talked to the seer,
giving him instructions where to travel until he and his people
came to the ocean. Then, after four years, the Lord came
down again in a cloud and instructed him to build a new kind
of barge in order to cross the great body of water. These
barges were not constructed in any manner understood today.
Instead they were built according to God's specifications. The
ships were as long as a tree and they were tightly made all
around so that water could not enter. For air, holes were
made in them in strategic points. In total, eight ships were
built.

The one problem they faced was that the design did not
allow light to enter into the ships. The brother of Jared
pointed out this fact to God who asked him what he should
prepare for the people to give them light. Spurred on by this
challenge, the prophet went up into the mountain and did
molten out of a rock sixteen small stones; and they were white
and clear, like transparent glass. He then took these stones to
God and he cried to the Lord, saying,

Look upon us with pity and suffer not that we shall go forth
across this raging deep in darkness; but behold these stones
which I have molten out of the rock. And I know, 0 Lord,
that you have all power, and can do whatsoever you wilt for
the benefit of man; therefore, touch these stones, 0 Lord,
with your finger, and prepare them that they may shine forth
in darkness; and they shall shine forth unto us in the vessels
which we have prepared, that we may have light while we
shall cross the sea. Behold Lord, you can do this. We know
that you art able to show forth great power, which looks
small unto the understanding of men.

When the seer said these words, the Lord stretched
forth his hand and touched the stones one by one with his
finger. And the veil was taken from off the eyes of the seer
and he saw the finger of the Lord; and it was like the finger of
a man, that is, flesh and blood. The seer fell down before the
Lord, for he was struck with fear. When the Lord saw that the
brother of Jared fell to the earth, the Lord said to him, "Arise,
why have you fallen?" And he answered the Lord, "I saw the
finger of the Lord, and I feared lest he should smite me; for I

knew not that the Lord had flesh and blood." The Lord responded to him, "Because of your faith you have seen that I shall take upon me flesh and blood; and never has man come before me with such exceeding faith as you have; for were it not so you could not have seen my finger. Did you see more than this?" And he answered, "No, Lord, show yourself to me." The Lord asked him, "Will you believe the words that I shall speak?" And the seer answered, "Yes Lord, I know that you speak the truth, for you are a God of truth, and cannot lie." When he had said these words, the Lord showed himself to him, and said,

> Because you know these things, you are redeemed from the fall; therefore, you are brought back into my presence; therefore, I show myself unto you. Behold, I am He who was prepared from the foundation of the world to redeem my people. Behold, I am Jesus Christ. I am the Father and the Son. In me shall all mankind have light, and that eternally even they who shall believe on my name; and they shall become my sons and my daughters. And never have I showed myself unto man whom I have created, for never has man believed in me as you have. See that you are created after mine own image? Yea, even all men were created in the beginning after mine own image. Behold, this body, which you now behold, is the body of my spirit; and man have I created after the body of my spirit, and even as I appear unto thee to be in the spirit will I appear unto my people in the flesh.

What a beautiful experience this prophet and seer had because of his immense faith in God. Jesus showed himself to this man in the spirit, even after the manner and likeness of the same body in which He appeared to many after His resurrection. The prophet no more needed faith, for he knew and doubted nothing. Having a perfect knowledge of God, he could not be kept from within the veil (the spiritual realm), and therefore he saw Jesus, long before He was born.

And the Lord said to him, "Behold, you shall not suffer these things which you have heard and seen to go forth into the world, until the time comes that I shall glorify my name in the flesh [Jesus' virgin birth, teachings, death and resurrection]. Therefore treasure up the things you have heard and seen, and write them and seal them up." Besides showing himself to the brother of Jared, the Lord showed him the inhabitants of the earth from the beginning to the end of time, and he also revealed to him many events that would transpire in the world. The brother of Jared recorded everything he saw and also included the *interpreters* with the record, because the record was sealed. Other prophets and seers read this record some years later (after the resurrection of Christ), and they testified that greater things had no man seen. The record was re-sealed and would not be read again until the latter days.

The colony now made preparations to enter the eight vessels and they placed two stones inside each vessel and these stones that the Lord caused to shine gave them light. They also took with them flocks, fowls, herds, animals, beasts, seeds of all kinds, and food for the animals and for themselves. After all the preparations were made, they entered the vessels and the Lord caused a strong wind to blow, thus causing them to drift toward the Promised Land (America). They sang praises of the Lord continually and were driven by the wind upon the waters for three hundred and forty-four days.

It seems that they landed upon the coast of Central America and when they set their feet upon the shores, they bowed themselves down upon the face of the land. There they humbled themselves before the Lord and shed tears of joy because of the multitude of His mercies over them. Afterwards, they went and began to till the earth. Thus began a great civilization in America.

As the years passed, the people began to spread out on the land and their population grew very quickly. There were times of blessings and times of terrible judgment. These times of judgment came when the Lord saw that sin was more prevalent than godliness. At those times, God sent prophets among them to declare many prophecies and to warn them of sin and transgression and their need to repent.

Down through the centuries kings were appointed, some good and some bad; and sometimes kings were overthrown by rebellious factions, causing wars and bloodshed for many years. At one point, secret groups were formed (called *secret combinations)* for the purpose of usurping (or seizing and controlling) the proper government and authorities. This usurpation was often performed through murder, intrigue, conspiracy or treachery. These groups used secret oaths or pacts handed down from Cain, the first murderer. Secret combinations (also called secret societies or secret associations) are abominable and wicked in the sight of God. They are used to gain power or wealth through illegal, unrighteous, unethical, or immoral means. Secret combinations, as well as pride, greed, lying, adultery and covetousness have all caused bloodshed and the destruction of many nations and people through the ages of time. Any nation that will uphold secret combinations to get power and gain will eventually be destroyed. Here is a prophecy from the Lord about us today:

> O ye gentiles [Americans], it is wisdom in God that these things should be shown unto you, that thereby you may repent of your sins, and suffer not that these murderous combinations shall get above you, which are built up to get power and gain – and the work, yea, even the work of destruction come upon you, yea, even the sword of the justice of the Eternal God shall fall upon you, to your overthrow and destruction if ye shall suffer these things to be. Wherefore the Lord commands you when you see these come upon you, that you shall awake to a sense of your awful situation, because of this secret combination [society] which shall be among you; and whoso builds it up seeks to overthrow the freedom of all lands, nations, and countries: and it brings to pass the destruction of all people, for it is built up by the devil, who is the father of all lies; even that same liar who beguiled our first parents. Yea, even that same liar who has caused man to commit murder from the beginning; who has hardened the hearts of men that they have murdered the prophets, and stoned them, and cast them out from the beginning.

The prophet was commanded to write these things that evil may be done away, and that the time may come that Satan may have no power upon the hearts of the children of men. Instead, they may be persuaded to continually do good, so that they can come unto the fountain of all righteousness and be saved.

As the years passed, the people would drift into sin so that divisions erupted; one faction fighting against another, kingdom against kingdom, civil strife and civil war, bloodshed, famine, and floods – all the judgments of God. When righteousness prevailed, they enjoyed great blessings of God -- fruits of all kinds including grain, silk, fine linens, gold, silver, and many other precious things. Even their herds and flocks were blessed. God poured out His blessings upon this land of America, choicest land above all others. Thus, a blessing and a curse was pronounced upon this land, depending on the inhabitants' spiritual status.

Faith in Christ is the victory, as the Apostle Paul said, "But without faith it is impossible to please him; for he that cometh to God must believe that He is, and that He is a rewarder of them that diligently seek him." Another ancient American prophet, sole survivor of the second migration and civilization, said, "Lord, the gentiles [Americans] shall mock at our words [Ancient Translated Nephite Record]." And the Lord answered the prophet, saying, "Fools mock, but they shall mourn."

Down through the centuries God sent many prophets, warning the descendants of the first colony of the judgments of God. By about 600 BC a prophet of God by the name of Ether had warned the inhabitants of the coming judgment of God upon them, because of sin and iniquity. A division took place and a great and final war began with millions of people fighting each other. Two great generals, one named Shiz and the other Coriantumr, gathered their respective people into two great armies. This process took four years. Everyone was armed with weapons, even women and children. Then they marched against each other. Thousands and thousands of them fought all day, but neither side was totally victorious.

Day after day the fighting continued, and more and more of them died. At night the survivors were weary and retired to their camps, where they began a howling and lamentation for the slain of their people; and so great were their cries, their howling and lamentations, that they shattered the night air. The spirit of the Lord ceased striving with them, and Satan had full power over the hearts of the people, for they were given-up to the hardness of their hearts, and the blindness of their minds, that they might be destroyed.

Every morning they again went to battle and many more were slain and finally there remained only fifty-two of the people of Coriantumr and sixty-nine of the people of Shiz. After resting at night again, they went to battle the next day, and there were left of the army of Shiz thirty-two and of the army of Coriantumr twenty-seven. This was truly a war of annihilation -- men, women, and children were killed. The few men that remained were large and mighty. After eating, sleeping, and resting they came to battle, and fought until two were left, Shiz and Coriantumr. Shiz fainted because of the loss of blood. Coriantumr rested a little, then he smote off the head of Shiz. Coriantumr lived to see the words of the Lord being fulfilled and he lived to see the migration of the third colony, which came to this land about 589 BC. Coriantumr lived among them for about nine months.

Thus, a great nation and a great civilization, that lasted 1600 years, was destroyed. The cause: iniquity and sin. Therefore, the judgments of God fell upon them. The prophet of God, Ether, survived this great catastrophe and the Lord spoke to him, saying, "Go forth." And he went forth and beheld the words of the Lord had all been fulfilled, and he finished the record and said, "The hundredth part I have not written." And he hid them in a manner that the second colony that came here about 600 BC, found the hidden plates. These plates or records give an account of the rise and fall of the first civilization in America.

I only gave a portion of the history in this writing. The last words that were written by Ether, the prophet who survived the great destruction, were these: "Whether the Lord will that I be translated, or that I suffer the will of the Lord in the flesh, it matters not, if it so be that I am saved in the Kingdom of God. Amen."

Chapter Nine

Second Migration to America

The second migration occurred about 600 BC. This colony was called the Lehi-Nephi expedition. Lehi, a prophet of God, lived in Jerusalem and was a contemporary of the prophet Jeremiah. Jeremiah discharged his Godly duties with unremitting diligence and fidelity during a course of at least forty-two years. He declared to the Jews the sin and transgressions that was among them and prophesied concerning their future captivity in Babylon. Many other prophets prophesied to the people that they must repent, or the great city of Jerusalem would be destroyed.

In the commencement of the first year of the reign of Zedekiah, King of Judah, the Prophet Lehi, who had dwelt at Jerusalem his entire life, told the Jews that they must repent of their abomination and sin or else perish by the sword and be carried to Babylon in captivity. He went to the Lord in prayer with all his heart on behalf of his people. And as he prayed, he saw a pillar of fire upon a rock before him; and he saw and heard many wondrous things. Because of these things, he did shake and tremble. Afterwards, he returned to his own house at Jerusalem and threw himself upon his bed. Being overcome with the Spirit, he was carried away in a vision and saw the heavens open and the Lord sitting upon His throne. He was surrounded with numberless concourses of angels who were singing and praising their God.

Lehi also saw someone descending out of the midst of heaven, and he beheld that this personage's luster was above that of the sun at noonday. Twelve others followed this personage (Jesus Christ), and their brightness did exceed that of the stars in the firmament. They came down and went forth upon the face of the earth. After seeing and hearing of the great and marvelous things, Lehi exclaimed,

> Great and marvelous are your works, O Lord God Almighty!
> Your throne is high in the heavens, and your power, goodness, and mercy are over all the inhabitants of the earth,

because You are merciful, You will not suffer those who come unto thee that they shall perish.

Lehi praised his God, for Lehi's soul rejoiced and his whole heart was filled with the Spirit of God, because of the things the Lord had shown him.

Lehi was married to Sariah and together they had four sons at Jerusalem. Beginning with the eldest, their names were: Laman, Lemuel, Sam, and Nephi. Lehi also had at least two daughters. The youngest son, Nephi, became a prophet and a leader of his people. God commanded Lehi and then Nephi to keep a record of their proceedings upon metal sheets (also known as plates). They were to record all of their dealings with God and their migration to the land of promise (America). Nephi also recorded their division, contentions, and wars. The metal he used was gold, thus this record was often called the *gold plates*. Nephi began his record thus,

I, Nephi, having been born of goodly parents, therefore, I was taught somewhat in all the learning of my father; and having seen many afflictions in the course of my days, nevertheless, having been highly favored of the Lord in all my days; yea, having had a great knowledge of the goodness and the mysteries of God, therefore I make a record of my proceedings in my days. Yea, I make a record in the language of my father, which consist of the learning of the Jews and the language of the Egyptians. And I know that the record I make is true. I make it with my own hands.

Lehi was commanded by the Lord to take his family and leave the city of Jerusalem and to journey through the wilderness. He was obedient to the commandments of the Lord. He left his home, his gold, silver, and all his precious things. Taking with him only provisions and tents, he traveled many days into the wilderness. The two elder sons murmured and complained to their father and refused to believe that Jerusalem would be destroyed according to the words of the prophets. They had a rebellious spirit, which was passed on to their posterity.

Camping in the wilderness closer to the Red Sea than others, Lehi was commanded by the Lord to send his sons back to Jerusalem to obtain the *record of the Jews*. This record had been kept for many generations and was maintained by a prominent and powerful Jew named Laban.

This record was kept on *brass plates*. On these plates (or sheets) were engraved the Hebrew Scriptures and genealogies, including many prophecies, such as Isaiah and Jeremiah. It was expedient and mandatory that Lehi and his family take this record with them for their journey to the land of promise (America). With these plates they would have a copy of the commandments of the Lord, the Law of Moses, the writings of the prophets, and a history of the world and the Jews. (I will also refer to this record as the *Jerusalem Brass Plates*.)

The four sons returned to Jerusalem, but it was young, faithful Nephi who obtained the plates (or record) from Laban. After returning to their father's camp, Lehi examined the plates and discovered that he was a descendant of **Joseph** who was sold by his brethren into Egypt. This fact is important to us as we show what the future holds for the American Indian.

Some may question why a descendent of Joseph was in Jerusalem. However, the Bible notes that "in Jerusalem dwelt of the children of Judah, and of the children of Benjamin, and of the children of Ephraim and Manasseh." As we know, Ephraim and Manasseh were the two sons of Joseph. (I would like to note that Laban, the record keeper, was also a descendant of Joseph.)

As an aside, during the process of obtaining the *Jerusalem Brass Plates,* an addition was made to Lehi's little colony. Laban's servant, Zoram, carried the plates to the walls of Jerusalem for Nephi. When he realized that Nephi was not Laban (Nephi had disguised himself), Zoram wanted to flee. But Nephi held him and promised that if he traveled with them into the wilderness, he could be a free man and not anyone's servant. Zoram accepted Nephi's offer. He went with the others as a free man and eventually became a close friend of Nephi.

Lehi was instructed to send his sons back to Jerusalem a second time. This time it was to convince a man by the name of Ishmael to take himself and his family into the wilderness to join Lehi. Ishmael had a wife, two sons and five daughters. His sons were also married. Ishmael decided to join the colony when Nephi and his brothers presented to him the words of the Lord. Nephi recorded that "the Lord softened the heart of Ishmael" insomuch that Ishmael and his family took their journey with Nephi and his brothers. The sons and daughters of these two families intermarried (particularly, one of Ishmael's daughters for each of Lehi's sons, while Zoram married the eldest daughter of Ishmael).

Nephi was commanded of the Lord to make two sets of gold plates or records. One was called the *small plates* and contained a sacred history plus prophecies and visions. The other set, the *large plates,* contained a secular (non-religious) history of the people. These plates were handed down from father to son and men of God through the centuries (from approximately 600 BC to AD 400) until the last two surviving prophets abridged them on to a separate set of gold plates. The abridgment was then buried in the ground where they remained until their location was revealed by a messenger of God to Joseph Smith, Jr. He then translated the record by the gift and power of God.

While Lehi and his colony were traveling through the wilderness, Nephi desired to see the things that God revealed to his father. Sometime between the years 600 and 592 BC the Lord took him up in the spirit and set him upon a high mountain. The spirit then said to the young prophet, "Do you believe all the things your father saw?" And he answered, "You know that I believe all the words of my father." And when he spoke these words, the spirit cried with a loud voice, saying, "Hosanna to the Lord, the most high God; for He is God over all the earth, yea above all. Blessed are you, because you believe in the Son of the most high God; wherefore, you shall behold the things you desire."

The spirit then told him to look and he saw a large and spacious field and a tree with fruit most desirable. A rod of iron lay on the bank of a river that led to the tree. The fruit was delicious and sweet and made one happy. The tree represented the tree of life, and the rod of iron the word of God. It was the same experience that his father was given.

The spirit in the form of an Angel then told him to look and he now saw Jerusalem and other cities in the future.

And I beheld the city of Nazareth, and in the city I saw a Virgin, she was exceedingly fair and white. And the Angel said, "Behold, the Virgin whom you see is the mother of the Son of God, after the manner of the flesh." Again he looked and he saw the Virgin bearing a child in her arms. Again he looked and he saw the Son of God going forth among the children of men; and many fell down at His feet and worshipped Him. Many were sick and afflicted with all manner of diseases, devils, and unclean spirits and were healed by the power of the Lamb of God. And he saw twelve others following Him [Apostles]. He saw Him taken by wicked hands and lifted up upon the cross, and slain for the sins of the world.

Now the Lord showed him the events that were to transpire hundreds of years into the future.

The Angel again said, "Look," and he looked and beheld many nations and kingdoms. The Angel said, "These are the nations and kingdoms of the gentiles [non-Israel]."

In this part of the vision he saw the migration of the gentile nations to the Western Hemisphere and American history foretold. Here it is. The young prophet said,

I beheld many waters [oceans] and they divided the gentiles from the posterity of my brethren [Native Americans]. And I looked and beheld a man among the gentiles [Columbus], who was separated from the descendants of my brothers, and I saw the spirit of God,[3] that it came down and wrought upon the man; and he went forth upon the many waters to the promised land [America and opening the way for the migration of the Gentile nations].

I beheld the spirit of God, that it wrought upon other gentiles [Pilgrims] and they went forth out of captivity, upon the many waters. And it came to pass that I beheld many multitudes of the gentiles upon the land of promise; and I beheld the wrath of God upon the seed of my brethren [Native Americans] and they were scattered before the gentiles and smitten [Indian wars].

I beheld the spirit of the Lord, that it was upon the gentiles, and they did prosper and obtain the land for their inheritance; and I beheld that they were white, and exceedingly fair and beautiful, like unto my people before they were slain. And I saw the gentiles [Puritans] had gone forth out of captivity and did humble themselves before the Lord, and the power of the Lord was with them. And I beheld that their mother gentiles [England] were gathered together upon the waters, and upon the land also, to battle against them [Revolutionary War]. And I beheld that the power of God was with them [Americans], and also that the wrath of God was upon all those that were gathered together against them to battle.

And I beheld that the gentiles who had gone out of captivity were delivered by the power of God out of the hands of all other nations. And I beheld that they did prosper in the land; and I beheld a book [Bible] was carried forth among them, and the Angel said, 'Do you know the meaning of the book?' And I said, 'I know not.' 'It proceeds from the mouth of a Jew, it is a record of the Jews, which contains the covenants of the Lord, for the house of Israel and gentiles. It contains many prophecies of the holy prophets. And it is a record like unto the engravings which are upon the plates of brass [the record obtained in Jerusalem] save they are not so many; nevertheless, they contain the covenants of the Lord.'

The angel further explained that the book (Bible), which the gentiles had, also contained the writings of the apostles. These writings were pure, however, because of the abominations of the gentiles, many plain and precious things were taken out of them. This removal was done so that it would pervert the right ways of the Lord, to blind and harden the hearts of men. (Again I want to remind you that this was given to the young prophet in a vision over twenty-five hundred years ago.)

Getting back to his vision; Nephi further explained that he saw the Gentiles who came to this land (America). He saw that they were lifted up by the power of God above all other nations. He was also told that America was a choice land, a land that the Lord had covenanted with Nephi's father to be the land of his posterity (Native Americans) for an inheritance.

The Angel of the Lord informed the young prophet concerning the words of Jesus Christ and described how he would manifest himself to Nephi's children. Also, the angel explained how they would write many things that Jesus would teach them. These writings were to be hid up in the earth (around AD 421) and would not come forth again until AD 1827. In that year, the record would be translated by the gift and the power of God.

And blessed are they who shall seek to bring forth my Zion at that day, for they shall have the gift and the power of the Holy Ghost; and if they endure until the end, they shall be lifted up at the last day, and shall be saved in, the everlasting kingdom of the Lamb.

Nephi also saw in the vision the Holy Bible and the Translated Ancient Nephite Records (Book of Mormon) taken to the Native Americans in the "latter days that they may learn of their origin and the covenants of God made to the house of Israel, and of their restoration to the land of their inheritance (America), and the restoration of the Jews and other tribes to the land of their inheritance (Canaan or what we call the Middle East)."

In the 37th chapter of Ezekiel, we read of two sticks or scrolls -- the stick of Judah (Bible) and the stick of Joseph (Ancient Nephite Record) that will become one in the hand of the God. The Ancient Nephite Records will establish the truth of the stick of Judah (Bible), and will make known many of the plain and precious things taken out of the Bible. And, more importantly, to make known to all kindred, tongues, and people, that the Lamb of God is the Son of the Eternal Father, and the Savior of the world, and that all men must come to him or they cannot be saved. Therefore, the Translated Ancient Nephite Record and the Holy Bible are one in the hand of the Lord, to establish the truth of the gospel of Jesus Christ.

The Angel spoke again to Nephi, saying,

> If the gentiles repent it shall be well with them: and you also know concerning the covenants made to the house of Israel; and you also have heard that whoso repents shall not perish. Therefore, woe unto the gentiles if it so be that they harden their hearts against the Lamb of God. For the time cometh, saith the Lamb of God, that I will work a great and a marvelous work among the children of men, a work which shall be everlasting, either on the one hand or the other – either to the convincing them unto peace and life eternal, or unto the deliverance of them to the hardness of their hearts and the blindness of their minds unto their being brought down to captivity, and also unto destruction, both temporally and spiritually, according to the captivity of the devil, of which I have spoken.

The young prophet also saw in a vision that there are truly only two churches; one is the church of the Lamb of God and the other the great and abominable church. Whoever does not belong to the church of the Lamb of God belongs to the great and abominable church. Nephi also saw that the numbers in the church of Jesus Christ were few because of the wickedness of the abominable church. The numbers in the abominable church were great among the gentile nations of the earth. And they united to fight against the Lamb of God. However, he said,

> I saw the power of the Lamb of God descend upon the Saints of the church of the Lamb, and upon the covenant people of the Lord, who were scattered upon all the face of the earth; and they were armed with righteousness and the power of God in great glory.

What a wonderful vision this young prophet experienced. His record of it provides insight into the future of Israel, the Native Americans and the gentiles of America, as well as the Church of Jesus Christ.

After many struggles and hardships, as well as many blessings from the Lord, the second colony traveled through the wilderness and reached the seashore. Lehi's wife, Sariah, bore two more sons during their journey through the wilderness. Their names were Jacob and Joseph. They arrived at the seashore about 592 BC. During the eight years in the wilderness there was much opposition from the two elder brothers, Laman and Lemuel. The Lord told Nephi to go up into the mountain and there the Lord spoke to him. He said to him, "You shall construct a ship, after the manner I shall show you that I may bring this people across these waters [ocean] to the land of promise [America]." Following the instructions of the Lord, they finally completed the ship, again after some opposition from the elder brothers who refused to believe in the works of the Lord and Nephi's ability to construct a ship. However, after its completion, they acknowledged that the workmanship was excellent, so they humbled themselves before the Lord.

The Lord was pleased with their efforts and humility, and commanded them to set sail for the Promised Land (America), taking with them meats, fruits, honey, and provisions according to the commandments of the Lord. They also took seeds of different kinds. Sailing for many days, crossing both the Indian and Pacific Oceans, the little Israelite colony finally landed on the west coast of America. The first thing they did was pitch their tents. They called their new home the Promised Land. They began to till the earth and plant the seeds that they brought from Jerusalem and they grew in abundance. And as they ventured into the new wilderness there were beasts of every kind, and all manner of animals for the use of man. And there was all manner of ore, such as gold, silver, and copper. Thus, ore was provided for the young prophet to make plates with engravings to record their history.

Between 588 BC and 570 BC Nephi explained the prophecies upon the *Jerusalem Brass Plates* concerning the scattering of the house of Israel among the nations and upon the face of the earth. After they shall be scattered and confounded, the Lord God would raise up a mighty nation (the United States) among the gentiles upon the Promised Land (America). And the Lord would proceed to do a marvelous work among them, which would be of great worth to the gentiles, and not only to them, but also to the house of Israel. And the Lord would make known to them His covenants that were made to Abraham, saying, "In your seed shall all the kindred of the earth be blessed." Wherefore, the Lord would bring them *again* out of captivity, and they would be gathered together to the lands of their inheritance; and they would be brought out of obscurity and out of darkness; and they would know that the Lord is their Savior and their Redeemer, the Mighty one of Israel. All who fight against Zion would be destroyed. For the time would come that the fullness of the wrath of God would be poured out upon all the children of men; for the Lord will not suffer that the wicked shall destroy the righteous, for He will preserve them by His power.

The prophet also explained that the time would speedily come that all churches that are built up to get gain, all of those that are built up to get power over the flesh, those that are built up to become popular in the eyes of the world, as well as those who seek the lust of the flesh and the things of the world, so that they may do all manner of iniquity, are they who need to fear, tremble, and quake for they must be brought low in the dust; they are those who must be consumed as stubble.

He further expounded that the time would hastily come that the righteous must be led up as calves of the stall, and the Holy One of Israel (Jesus Christ) must reign in dominion, might, power, and great glory. And He shall gather His children from the four quarters of the earth, and there will be one fold and one shepherd. Behold, all nations, kindred, tongues

45

and people shall dwell safely in the Holy One of Israel if they repent.

Around 570 BC, contention arose among the people. The two elder brothers (Laman and Lemuel), who were constantly rebelling against their father (Lehi), sought to take the life of their younger brother (Nephi) who was their spiritual and natural leader.

The Lord warned Nephi to flee into the American wilderness. He took his family, Zoram (Laban's former servant) and his family, one elder brother (Sam) and his family, two younger brothers (Jacob and Joseph), his sisters, and all of those who believed in the warnings and revelations of God. After traveling for many days, they pitched their tents in a place and called it after the name of the prophet, Nephi.

Now all of those who went with him took the name of Nephi, or the Nephite people. And they observed the judgments, statutes, and commandments of the Lord in all things according to the Law of Moses. The Lord blessed them and they prospered exceedingly. They sowed various types of seeds and reaped great harvests. They raised all kinds of flocks and animals. Nephi, as their leader, had the *Jerusalem Brass Plates* (the Hebrew Scriptures and history that Nephi brought from Jerusalem) as well as the *American Gold Plates* (the records Nephi was commanded to start and generally called the *Plates of Nephi*).

The Nephites began to multiply quickly in their new homeland. Nephi taught them how to make swords for protection against his two elder brothers and their people (who were now called Lamanites). The Lamanites would attack the Nephites because of their hatred for them and believing that Nephi had improperly taken command of the journey to the Promised Land and had chosen himself to be their king. They ignored how God had selected Nephi and performed many mighty works through him, even saving Laman and Lemuel's lives. The Lamanites also believed that Nephi had undeservedly taken the records from them, even though God had commanded Nephi to obtain the *Jerusalem Brass Plates* and make the *American Gold Plates*.

Nephi encouraged his people to be industrious and to build buildings, work with all kinds of materials and metals, all of which were in abundance. They built a temple after the manner of Solomon, except without the material that Solomon had, however, the workmanship was excellent.

Because of their iniquity, unbelief and idolatry, the Lamanites were cut off from the presence of the Lord, that is, the Spirit of God did not work with them. As a consequence of this condition, God changed their complexion and customs from fair and delightsome to blackness and loathsome. He did this act so that the Lamanites were distinguishable from the Nephites and that the Nephites would not associate with them. The Lamanites also became an idle people, full of mischief, and hunted in the wilderness for beasts of prey. And the Nephites who mixed with the Lamanites became like the Lamanites. Within the next ten years, the two nations contended and warred with each other (brother against brother).

The two youngest sons of Lehi, who had gone with Nephi, Jacob and Joseph, were ordained and consecrated as priests and teachers by Nephi, so that they might teach the people the commandments of God. Jacob began to teach his people concerning the temporal and spiritual death, salvation, and the resurrection. He said,

> I know and you know that our flesh must waste away and die; nevertheless, in our bodies we shall see God. You also know that the Messiah shall show himself in Jerusalem and suffers himself to become subject unto man in the flesh and die for all men, that all men might become subject unto him. [This was revealed to the prophets about 560 BC.] For as death has passed upon all men to fulfill the merciful plan of the great Creator, there must needs be a power of resurrection, and the resurrection must need to come unto man by reason of the fall; and the fall came by reason of transgression; and because men became fallen they were cut off from the presence of the Lord. Wherefore, it must need be an infinite atonement-except it be an infinite atonement this corruption could not put on incorruption. Wherefore, the first judgment which came upon man must need to have remained to an endless duration. And if so, this flesh must have lain down to rot and to crumble to its mother earth, to rise no more.
>
> Oh the wisdom of God, his mercy and grace! For behold, if the flesh should rise no more our spirits must become subject to that angel who fell from the presence of the Eternal God, and became the devil, to rise no more. And our spirits become like his, angels to a devil, to be shut out from the presence of our God, and to remain with the father of lies, in

misery like himself, yes, to that being who beguiled our first parents, who transformed himself nigh into an angel of light, and stirs up the children of men into secret combinations of murder and all manner of secret works of darkness.

Oh how great the goodness of our God, who prepares a way for our escape from the grasp of that awful monster; yea, that monster, death and hell, which I call the death of the body, and also the death of the spirit. And because of the way of deliverance of our God, the Holy One of Israel, this death, of which I have spoken, which is the temporal, shall deliver up its dead; which death is the grave. And this death of which I have spoken, the spiritual death shall deliver up its dead; which spiritual death is hell. Wherefore death and hell must deliver up their dead. Hell must deliver up its captive spirits. The grave must deliver up its captive bodies, and the bodies and the spirits of men will be restored one to the other; it is by the power of the resurrection of the Holy one of Israel [the Messiah].

Oh how great the plan of our God! For on the other hand, the Paradise of God must deliver up the spirits of the righteous, and the grave deliver up the body of the righteous; and the spirit and the body is restored to itself again, and all men become incorruptible, immortal, and they are living souls, having a perfect knowledge like unto us in the flesh, except it be that our knowledge shall be perfect.

Wherefore, we shall have a perfect knowledge of all our guilt, and our uncleanness, and our nakedness; and the righteous shall have a perfect knowledge of their enjoyment, their righteousness, being clothed with purity, even with the robe of righteousness. And when all men shall pass from the first death unto life, insomuch as they have become immortal, they must appear before the judgment-seat of the Holy One of Israel and be judged according to the holy judgment of God.

And assuredly, as the Lord lives, for the Lord God had spoken it, and it is His eternal word, which cannot pass away, that they who are righteous shall be righteous still, and they who are filthy shall be filthy still. Wherefore, they who are filthy are of the devil and his angels; they shall go away into everlasting fire prepared for them, and their torment is as a lake of fire and brimstone, whose flame, ascends up forever and ever and has no end.

Oh the greatness and justice of our God, for He executes all of His words. They have gone forth out of His mouth, and his law must be fulfilled. But behold, the righteous, the Saints of the Holy One of Israel, they who have believed in the Lord and have endured the crosses of the world, and despised the shame of it, shall inherit the kingdom of God, which was prepared from the foundation of the world, and their joy shall be full forever.

Oh the greatness and mercy of our God and His holiness, for He knows all things. And He came into the world that he may save all men if they will hearken unto His voice. He suffered the pains of all creatures that belong to the family of Adam. He commanded that all men must repent and be baptized in His name, having perfect faith in the Lord or they cannot be saved in the kingdom of God. And if they will not repent and be baptized and endure until the end, they must be damned, for the Lord has spoken it.

Jacob, continued to exhort the word of the Lord, including some warnings, saying,

Woe unto the rich, who are rich as to the things of the world. Because they are rich they despise the poor, and they persecute the meek; their hearts are upon their treasures; wherefore, their treasure is their god. And behold, their treasure shall perish with them.

And woe unto the deaf, for they shall perish. Woe unto the blind that will not see, for they shall perish also. Woe unto the uncircumcised of heart, for a knowledge of their iniquities shall smite them at the last day. Woe unto the liar, for he shall be thrust down to hell. Woe unto the murderer who deliberately kills, for he shall die. Woe unto them who commit whoredoms, for they shall be thrust down to hell. And woe unto those who worship idols, for the devil of all devils delights in them. And in fine, woe unto all those who die in their sins; for they shall return to God, and behold His face, and remain in their sins.

The prophet continued by saying,

Oh, my beloved brethren, remember the awfulness in transgressing against the Holy God, and also the awfulness of yielding to the enticings of that cunning one. Remember, to be carnally minded is death, and to be spiritually minded is life eternal. Oh my beloved brethren, give ear to my words.

He also received messages from angels regarding the coming of Christ, as follows:

An Angel spoke to me and informed me that a redeemer is to come and his name shall be Christ. He will come among His own people and they shall reject Him [with the exception of a few]. And because of priest crafts and iniquities, they at Jerusalem will be against Him, and crucify Him. Destructions, famines, pestilence, and bloodshed shall come upon them; and they who shall not be destroyed shall be scattered among all nations.

But behold, thus saith the Lord God: When the day comes that they shall believe in me, that I am Christ [Messiah], then have I covenanted with their fathers that they shall be restored in the flesh, upon the earth, unto the lands of their inheritance. And it shall come to pass that they shall be gathered in from their long dispersion, from the isles of the sea and from the four corners of the earth.

Fifty-five years passed from the time Lehi's colony left Jerusalem. During that time, Ishmael died and then a number of years later Lehi died. Finally, Nephi died. A new king was selected from among the people, but he took the name Nephi in honor of their first king. Both the Nephites and the Lamanites increased in population very rapidly. The Nephites, however, continued to be very industrious in all things, and greatly added to their wealth.

After the death of Nephi, his brother Jacob gathered the people to the temple and preached the following words to them.

It grieves me that I must use boldness of speech concerning you, because of your wickedness among you. The Lord has commanded me to declare unto you these words. And now, behold, my brethren, many of you have begun to search for gold, silver, and all manner of precious ore in which this land abounds. And many of you have become rich more so than your brethren, and are lifted up in the pride of your hearts; wear stiff necks and high heads because of the costliness of your apparel, and persecute your brethren because you suppose that you are better than they. Do you suppose that God justifies you in this thing? No, He condemns you, and if you persist in these things, His judgments must swiftly come upon you. Before you seek for riches, *seek for the kingdom of God* and let not the pride of your hearts destroy your souls.

Jacob continued his sermon by approaching a more sensitive sin.

I spoke to you concerning this pride. But I must speak to you of a grosser crime. The word of God burdens me because of this grosser crime. For behold, thus saith the Lord: 'This people begin to wax in iniquity, for they do not understand the scriptures, for they seek to excuse themselves in committing whoredoms, because of the things which were written concerning David, and Solomon, his son.

Behold, David and Solomon truly had many wives and concubines, which thing was **abominable** before me,' saith the Lord. 'I have led this people out of the land of Jerusalem, by the power of my arm that I might raise up unto me a righteous branch from the posterity of Joseph, who was sold by his brethren into Egypt. Therefore, I the Lord God will not suffer that this people shall do like unto them of old. My brethren hear me, and hearken to the word of the Lord: **for there shall not any man among you have save it be ONE wife; and concubines he shall have none, for I the Lord God delight in the chastity of women.** And whoredoms are an abomination before me.' Thus says the Lord of Hosts, 'This people shall keep my commandments or cursed be the land for their sakes.' [Emphasis added by author.]

For I the Lord have seen the sorrow, and heard the mourning of the daughters of my people in the land of Jerusalem, and in all the lands of my people, because of the wickedness and abominations of their husbands. I will not suffer the cries of the fair daughters of this people, which I have led out of the land of Jerusalem. For they shall not lead away captive the daughters of my people because of their tenderness, except I shall visit them with a sore curse, even unto destruction; for they shall not commit whoredoms, like them of old,' saith the Lord.

You have broken the hearts of your tender wives, and lost the confidence of your children, because of your bad examples before them. And the sobbings of their hearts ascend up to God against you. And because of the strictness of the word of God, which comes down against you, many hearts died, pierced with deep wounds.

Jacob also pointed out to them the following irony about their dark-skinned brothers, who were cursed because of their religious disbelief, but who would be forever blessed because of one particular good work.

Behold, the Lamanites your brethren, whom ye hate because of their filthiness and the cursing which has come upon their skins are more righteous than you; for they have not forgotten the commandment of the Lord, which was given unto our fathers – that they should have save it were **one wife** and concubines they should have none. Behold, their husbands love their wives, and their wives love their husbands and their husbands and their wives love their children. Wherefore, ye shall remember your children, how that ye have grieved their hearts because of the example that ye have set.

What a wonderful message for today, some 2500 years later; husbands and wives loving each other and setting a good example for children. Today we need to re-establish the importance of the family, even as God had designed it. Jesus Christ confirmed this when he said that God made us male and female and that a man should leave his mother and father and cleave to his wife and the two should be one. The Apostle Paul said that a husband should love his wife as much as Jesus loves the Church, for whom He died.

Dear reader, understand that marriage and family was instituted by God and He loves to see families living in peace and harmony following the teachings of His son, with no adultery, no fornication, and no abuse (wife or child).

Jacob noted that God would bless the Lamanites for this one thing that they did right. His words were: "In keeping this commandment, the Lord God will not destroy them, but will be merciful unto them and one day they shall become a blessed people." What a beautiful promise. We need to take heed of this promise. Although the Lamanites did many things wrong, God considered their family love ideal.

Jacob continued his record (on the gold plates) by stating,

I, Jacob, having ministered much unto my people in word (I cannot write but a little of my words, because of the difficulty of engraving our words upon plates), we know the things we write upon plates must remain, which will give our children and our brethren a small degree of knowledge concerning us and their fathers. And for this intent have we written these things, that they may know that we knew of Christ, and we had a hope of His glory many hundred years before His coming; not only we ourselves had a hope of His glory, but also all the holy prophets who were before us.

Worshipping the great Jehovah in the name of the Messiah [Christ], we also worship the Father in His name. And for this intent we keep the law of Moses, it *pointing* our souls to Him; for this cause it is sanctified unto us for righteousness, even as it was accounted unto Abraham in the wilderness to be obedient unto the commands of God in offering up his son Isaac, which is a similitude of God and His Only Begotten Son.

The Lord God shows us our weakness by His grace. Great and marvelous are the works of the Lord. How unsearchable are the depths of the mysteries of Him; and it is impossible that man should find out all His ways. No man knows of His ways except it is revealed to him; wherefore, brethren, despise not the revelations of God.

Beloved brethren, be reconciled unto Him through the atonement of Christ, His Only Begotten Son, and you may obtain a resurrection, according to the power of the resurrection which is in Christ, as the first fruits of Christ unto God. The Holy Spirit speaks the truth, as they really are; and of things as they really will be.

After some years passed away there came a man among the Nephites who declared that there should be no Christ. He preached many things that were flattering to the people. He acted this way so that he might destroy the doctrine of Christ and lead away many hearts. He knew that Jacob had faith in the coming of Christ and he sought an opportunity to challenge Jacob. He was a learned man, and had a perfect knowledge of the people's language; he could use much flattery and power of speech, according to the power of the devil. He hoped to shake Jacob from his faith, not understanding the many revelations and the many things Jacob had seen. For Jacob truly had seen Angels, and they ministered to him. He also heard the voice of the Lord from time to time; therefore, his faith could not be shaken.

53

Eventually the opportunity came for this *antichrist* to meet Jacob. He said, 'Brother Jacob, I was waiting for an opportunity to speak to you, for I have heard and know that you go about preaching the gospel or the doctrine of Christ. You have led away many of these people that they pervert the right way of God and do not teach the law of Moses and interpret the law of Moses into a being which you say shall come hundreds of years from now and behold, I declare unto you that this is blasphemy; for no man knows of such things; for he cannot tell of things to come.' And in this manner did the man contend with the prophet.

Jacob wrote his reaction and response to the man. He said, "The Lord God poured out His spirit into my soul, that I confounded him in all his words. And I said to the unbelieving man, 'Do you deny the Christ who should come?' And he said, 'If there be a Christ, I would not deny Him; but I know there is no Christ.' And I said, 'Do you believe the scriptures?' And he said, 'Yes.' 'Then you do not understand them; for they truly testify of Christ. And it has been made manifested to me by the power of the Holy Ghost, and if there be no atonement made, all mankind must be lost.' And the unbelieving man said, "Show me a sign by this Holy Ghost in which you know so much." And the prophet said to him, "Who am I that I should tempt the Lord to show you a sign, in which you know to be true? You will deny it, because you are of the evil spirit. Nevertheless, not my will be done; but if God shall smite you, let that be a sign to you that he has power both in heaven and on earth and also that Christ shall come. And your will O Lord be done, and not mine."

And when the prophet had spoken these words, the power of the Lord came upon the man insomuch that he fell to the earth, and he was nursed many days. Finally he said to the people, "Gather on the morrow for I shall die, and I desire to speak to you before I die." So the next day they gathered together and he denied the things he spoke to them concerning the Christ, saying that he was deceived by the power of the devil. "There is a Christ coming, there is the power of the Holy Ghost and the ministering of Angels." And he also spoke of hell, and of eternity and eternal punishment. And he said, "I fear that I have committed the unpardonable sin, for I have lied unto God, I denied the Christ and the scriptures." After he had spoken these words, he died. And when the people witnessed this, the power of God came down upon them. Peace and the love of God were again restored among them.

Over the years, means were devised by the Nephites to restore the Lamanites, who had become their enemies, to the knowledge of the truth. The Lamanites, on the other hand, sought by physical strength to destroy the Nephites at every opportunity. By this time, Jacob was quite old and was soon to go the way of all flesh, so he gave charge of the records to his son. His last words were, "And to the reader I say farewell, brethren, adieu [i.e., 'I commend you to God']." And he died.

As the years passed by there were many wars and contentions. The Nephites were considered the people of God, knowing the commandments of God, having the Law of Moses and the Jewish scriptures down through the Prophet Jeremiah upon the *Jerusalem Brass Plates* they brought with them. Yet there were times they transgressed and sin abounded. Around 130 BC a Nephite was warned of God to take all of those who believed in the things of God and flee into the wilderness. His name was Mosiah. As they traveled through the American wilderness, they discovered the **third colony** living north of their land.

Chapter Ten

Third Migration To America

The third colony came from Jerusalem about 589 BC. Among them was the son of King Zedekiah, king of Jerusalem. The king had been taken prisoner when the Babylonians besieged Jerusalem. God led this third colony out of Jerusalem with one of Zedekiah's sons. We shall call this third colony the *Mulekites,* after the name of Zedekiah's son Mulek. Mulek was not slain with his brothers, but escaped from Jerusalem, as was prophesied by Isaiah and Ezekiel.[4] One of the interesting features of this colony is that we do not know the other members of the group, or any of their travels, except that God led them to America. They also did not keep records like Lehi's colony.

When the Mulekites arrived in America they lived for many years away from the other colonies until Mosiah of the Nephites (second colony) discovered them. They had lost all knowledge of God and the Jewish scriptures. At times they had civil war, and even their language became corrupted. Both of these problems occurred because they brought no records with them. However, the Nephites taught them their language and the scriptures.

At the time of their discovery by Mosiah, a man named Zarahemla led the Mulekites. They called their land *Zarahemla* and they called themselves the *People of Zarahemla.* These people rejoiced when Mosiah and his people discovered them, especially when they learned that Mosiah had the records from Jerusalem. They united as one people and Mosiah was selected to be their king.

Zarahemla, after learning Mosiah's language, told Mosiah his genealogy. He also told about a large stone that was found with foreign engravings on it. Mosiah, by the gift and power of God, interpreted the engravings. The engravings were a record that gave an account of Coriantumr and his slain people (see the end of Chapter 8), as well as how his forefathers had come to America at the time of the confounding of the languages (Tower of Babel). The record also told of the severity of the Lord's judgment upon them and how their bones laid scattered in the land north of Zarahemla.

The impact of these two people uniting was felt for many years after. The Nephites' capital city became Zarahemla and remained so for over a hundred years. The unification of the two groups allowed them to defend themselves against the Lamanites. (Unfortunately, we do not yet fully know what the full significance of the third colony to America was or will be. However, the prophecy of Isaiah found in 2 Kings 19:30-31 states, "And the remnant that is escaped of the house of Judah shall yet again take root downward, and bear fruit upward. For out of Jerusalem shall go forth a remnant, and they that escape out of mount Zion: the zeal of the LORD of hosts shall do this.") At this juncture, I will now relate the history of the combined people, who I will refer to as the Nephites.

Mosiah was a good and righteous king, and he conferred the kingdom upon his son, Benjamin. Benjamin was a holy man and he too reigned over his people with righteousness. There were also holy men, who spoke with the power and authority of God. They eventually established peace in the land and for a time, brought an end to the wars with the Lamanites.

When Benjamin was quite old and recognized that he would soon die, he made a proclamation that all the people in the land should gather together to hear his final words of exhortation, as well as his conferring the kingdom on his son Mosiah (Mosiah II). King Benjamin used a large and high tower for his address (and for those who could not hear, the address was written and distributed among them). The people who assembled at the tower offered sacrifices and burnt offerings according to the law of Moses, to give thanks to the Lord who brought them out of bondage in the land of Egypt, and the same God who brought them to the Promised Land (America) by His power.

The people had also pitched tents around the tower, every man according to his family, consisting of his wife, sons, daughters, and their grandchildren from the eldest to the youngest. They had the door of their tents open so that many of them could hear the king's address. The following is an excerpt of the words he spoke and wrote:

My brethren, all of you who have assembled yourselves together, you who can hear my words which I shall speak unto you this day; for I have not commanded you to come up here to trifle with the words which I shall speak, but that you should hearken unto me, and open your hearts that you may understand the mysteries of God to be unfolded to you. I have not commanded you to come up here to fear me. I myself am not more than a mortal man. I am like yourselves, subject to all manner of infirmities in the body and mind. I have been consecrated to be a ruler and a king by the hand of the Lord to serve you with all my might, strength, and mind which the Lord had granted unto me. I have suffered to spend my days in your service, even up to this time. I have not sought gold, silver, or any manner of riches from you.

How impressive this king was! If we could only have such men in our governments – not only in the United States but in all the nations and kingdoms of the world!

The king continued his speech, saying:

Neither have I suffered that you should be confined in dungeons, nor that you should make slaves one of another, nor that you should murder, plunder, steal, or commit adultery, nor to commit any manner of wickedness. I have taught you that you should keep the commandments of the Lord, in all things which he has commanded you. And even I myself have labored with my own hands that I might serve you, and that you should not be laden with burdensome taxes or anything come upon you that which is grievous to be borne – and to all these things I have spoken you yourselves are witnesses this day.

Yet, my brethren, I have not done these things that I might boast, nor to accuse you; but I tell you these things that you may know that I can answer with a clear conscience before God this day. Behold, because I said to you I spent all my days in your service, I do not desire to boast, for I have only been in the service of God. And I tell you these things that you may learn wisdom; that you may learn that when you are in the service of your fellow men, you are only in the service of your God. And now if I whom you call your king has spent my days in your service, then should you not labor to serve one another? And oh how you ought to thank your heavenly king.

And if you will serve Him that created you from the beginning, and is preserving you from day to day, by giving you breath that you may live, move, and do according to your own will. And what He requires of you is to keep His commandments and you shall prosper in the land and be bless you. As you were created from the dust of the earth, I, your king, am no better than you are, for I am also created of the dust of the earth. I am getting old and am about to give up this mortal frame to the mother earth. And that I might be found blameless, free from the blood of all men, with a clear conscience, I will go to my grave in peace and my immortal spirit may join the choirs above in singing the praises of a just God.

A few more things I wish to tell you before I leave this world and confer the kingship upon my son, Mosiah. The Angel of the Lord came to me and said, 'Awake, and hear the words which I shall tell thee; for behold, I am come to declare unto you the glad tidings of great joy. The Lord had heard your prayers and has judged your righteousness and sent me to declare these things that you may have joy and declare it unto your people that they also may be filled with joy.

Behold, the time soon comes that the Messiah shall come among the children of men and shall work mighty miracles, such as healing the sick, raising the dead, causing the lame to walk, the blind to receive their sight, and the deaf to hear, and curing all manner of diseases. He shall cast out devils, or evil spirits which dwell in the hearts of men. He shall suffer temptations, pain of body, hunger thirst, and fatigue and blood from every pore, so great shall be his anguish for the wickedness and the abominations of the people. And this Messiah shall be called the Son of God and his mother shall be called Mary. He comes that salvation might come to the children of men.' Now I have spoken the words which the Angel had told me.

Here the Angel of the Lord had revealed to the king the name of the Savior and His mother's name, as well as the plan of salvation one hundred and twenty-four years before the birth of Christ. Not only that, Benjamin learned about Jesus' ministry to those afflicted with diseases and evil spirits, and how He would pour out his soul for the welfare of mankind.

King Mosiah II began to reign in his father's place at the age of thirty. He too walked in the ways of the Lord, and observed his judgments and statutes, and kept the commandments. He encouraged his people to continue tilling the earth even as he did, that he might follow his father's example and teachings. And there was no contention among all his people and they were at peace with the Lamanites. Besides being a good king, Mosiah II was also a prophet and a seer.

A group wanted to make an expedition to the original land of Nephi to where some Nephites had gone during the reign of Mosiah's grandfather. During their exploration, they not only found a group of Nephites, but these Nephites had discovered a land covered with the bones of people and beasts, and ruins of buildings of every kind. The explorers brought back with them *twenty-four plates of pure gold* with unreadable engravings upon them. They presented the plates to King Mosiah II. As a seer, he was able to translate the engravings by the gift and power of God. The result of the translation was the history of the first colony (2200 BC to about 550 BC) and their eventual annihilation by civil war. This discovery brought all of the migrations together (although only the first migration by their record).

As time went on, fierce wars once again erupted between the Nephites and the Lamanites. Down through the generations the unbelieving attitude and rebellious spirit of the Lamanites was transmitted to their posterity. Losing knowledge of the true, living God, they fought against the Nephites, whose advancement and decline depended upon their spiritual status. There was much suffering and bloodshed between the two great nations that now existed in Ancient America.

Around 148 BC a man by the name of Alma was converted by a prophet who preached concerning the coming of the Messiah (Jesus). Having faith in God and the coming of Christ, Alma began to preach about Christ and the resurrection. He obtained the authority from God and the king to establish churches throughout the land, and was called to the office of High Priest. However, there were many people who refused to believe and thus a division developed among the Nephites, placing them in jeopardy of God's judgments. Alma had received, by revelation, the authority to baptize. Those who believed and repented were baptized. (Here baptism was practiced before the coming of Christ by revelation, similar to John the Baptist, who was baptizing before the coming of Christ.)

I would like to take a few moments and talk about Jesus and his baptism. When Jesus came to John the Baptist who was His second cousin, to be baptized, John refused, recognizing Jesus as the *Lamb of God* who would take away the sins of the world: the *Messiah* and *Savior.* But Jesus said to him, "Suffer it to be so now: for thus it becomes us to fulfill all righteousness." And so John baptized Jesus by immersion. Afterwards, Jesus came out of the water and the heavens were opened to him, and he saw the Spirit of God descending like a dove, lighting upon him. A voice from heaven said, "This is my beloved Son, in whom I am well-pleased."

Jesus did not need baptism, but he humbled himself to baptism to set an example and to fulfill the plan of salvation. Thus, it is essential that all men and women believe and have faith in Christ and are baptized, by one with authority, for the remission of sins. After baptism, they must remain faithful (endure) to the end of their lives so that they can be saved. Jesus told a man named Nicodemus, a ruler of the Jews, "Verily, verily, I say unto thee, except a man be born of water and of the Spirit, he cannot enter into the Kingdom of God."

Now, let's return to our account of the High Priest Alma. The unbelievers began a great persecution against the people of God, so the king sent out a proclamation through the land, saying, "That there should be no persecution among them, but there should be an equality among all men; they should not let pride nor haughtiness disturb their peace; that every man should esteem his neighbor as himself, laboring with their own hand for their support. And all their priests and teachers should labor with their own hands for their support, except in cases where there is sickness or in want, doing these things that they may abound in grace."

Among the unbelievers was the son of the prophet and High Priest whose name was also Alma (whom we will call Alma II) and four sons of King Mosiah II. They greatly hindered the advancement of the church by their improper and unseemly actions. Alma prayed with great faith for his unbelieving son and the Lord answered his prayer. As his son and the sons of the king were going about rebelling against God, behold, the Angel of the Lord appeared unto them; and he descended as it were in a cloud; and he spoke as it were with a voice of thunder, which caused the earth to shake where they stood. And so great was their astonishment that they fell to the earth. At first they didn't understand the angel's words. The angel spoke to them again, saying, "Arise, why do you persecute the church of God? For the Lord has said, 'This is my Church, I will establish it; and nothing shall overthrow it, except the transgression of my people.'" And again, the angel said,

> Behold, the prayers of His people, and also the prayers of His servant, your father; for he has prayed with much faith concerning you that you might be brought to the knowledge of the truth; therefore, for this purpose have I come to convince you of the power and authority of God, that the prayers of His servants might be answered according to their faith.

> And behold, can you dispute the power of God? For behold, does not my voice shake the earth? And can you not also behold me before you? And I am sent from God. Now go, and remember the captivity of your fathers and the great things He had done for them. I say unto you, go your way, and do not seek to destroy the church any more.

These were the last words the angel spoke to them. Alma II and those who were with him fell to the earth again, so great was their astonishment; for with their own eyes they had beheld an angel of the Lord; and his voice was as thunder, which shook the earth; and they knew that there was nothing except the power of God that could shake the earth and cause it to tremble as though it would part asunder.

The astonishment of Alma II was greater than his friends and he became dumb and very weak so that he could not move his limbs. He was taken by his friends and carried helpless and laid before his father. And they rehearsed for his father all that had happened to them. His father rejoiced, for he knew that it was the power of God. He even caused the multitude to gather together that they might witness what the Lord had done for his son, and also for those that were with him. He caused the servants of the Lord to assemble themselves together; and they began to fast and pray to the Lord their God that He would open the mouth of Alma II and that his limbs might receive their strength and that the eyes of the people might be opened to see and know of the goodness and glory of God.

After they had fasted and prayed for the space of two days and two nights, the limbs of Alma II received their strength, and he stood up and began speaking to them to be of good comfort. And he said unto them, "I have repented of my sins, and have been redeemed of the Lord; behold, I am born of the spirit, and the Lord said marvel not that all mankind, yea men and women, all nations, kindred, tongues and people, must be born again; yea be born of God, changed from their carnal and fallen state, to a state of righteousness, being redeemed of God, becoming his sons and daughters. Thus they become new creatures; and unless they do this, they can in nowise inherit the kingdom of God."

This unbelieving young man who had repented, said,

> This must be the case or else you must be cast off; and this I know, because I was like to be cast off. Nevertheless, after wandering through much tribulation, repenting nigh unto death, the Lord in mercy had seen fit to snatch me out of an everlasting burning, and I am born of God. My soul had been redeemed from the gall of bitterness and bonds of iniquity. I was in the darkest abyss; but now I behold the marvelous light of God. My soul was racked with eternal torment; but I am snatched, and my soul is pained no more. I rejected my Redeemer, and denied that which had been spoken of by our fathers;

> But now that they may foresee that He will come, and that he remembers every creature of His creating, He will make himself manifest unto all. Yes, every knee shall bow, and every tongue confesses before Him. Yes, even at the last day, when all men shall stand to be judged of Him, then shall they confess, who live without God in the world, that the judgment of an everlasting punishment is just upon them; and they shall quake, and tremble, and shrink beneath the glance of His all searching eye.

The young man repented of his evil life, along with the four sons of the king and from that time forward, they began to repair the damage they had done. They traveled round about through all the land, publishing to all the people the things which they had heard and seen, and preaching the word of God in much tribulation, being greatly persecuted by those who were unbelievers, being smitten by many of them. They were a consolation to the church, confirming the faith of the members, and exhorting them with long-suffering and much travail to keep the commandments of God.

So they were instruments in the hands of God in bringing many to the knowledge of the truth, yes, to the knowledge of their Redeemer. They published peace; they published good tidings of good; and they declared to the people that the Lord God reigns.

Chapter Eleven

A Nation Flourishes in Ancient America

About 92 BC the prophet and High Priest Alma I died at the age of eighty-two. He consecrated his son Alma II to be High Priest, conferring the power and authority he received from God on his son. At this time King Mosiah desired to confer the kingship upon one of his sons. However, each of his four sons refused to accept it. Their desire was to preach righteousness and peace to the Lamanites. The sons of the King believed that through the preaching of the word of God, the wars and contentions could be brought to an end. The king therefore said,

> Let us appoint judges, to judge this people according to our law; and we will newly arrange the affairs of this people, for we will appoint wise men to be judges who will judge this people according to the commandments of God. Therefore, choose you by the voice of this people, judges, that you may be judged according to the laws which have been given you by our fathers, which are correct, and which were given them by the hand of the Lord.

> Now it is not common that the voice of the people desires anything contrary to that which is right; but it is common for the lesser part of the people to desire that which is not right; therefore, this shall be observed and make it your law-to do your business by the voice of the people.

Here in Ancient America a form of democracy was established after many years of governing by monarchies.

> And if the time comes that the voice of the people chooses iniquity, then is the time that the judgments of God will come upon you; then is the time He will visit you with great destruction. And if you have judges who do not judge you according to the law, which has been given, you can have them judged by a higher judge. If your higher judges do not judge righteous judgments, then a small number of your lower judges should get together and judge your higher

judges, according to the voice of the people. And I command you to do these things in the fear of the Lord.

And I desire that inequality should be no more in this land, especially among my people. I desire that this land [America] be a land of liberty, and every man may enjoy his rights and privileges alike, as long as the Lord sees fit. And to all nations of people that may possess this land. And when the inhabitants of this land [America] become ripened in sin, abominations, and iniquities, the judgments of God shall strike.

Alma II, the new High Priest, was also elected the first Chief Judge. This meant that he had charge over the administrative affairs of the people of Nephi, as well as their spiritual affairs. Alma II walked in the ways of the Lord and kept His commandments and made righteous judgments. So now the Nephites entered *the era of judges* throughout all the land of Zarahemla. A few years after the establishment of judges, old King Mosiah, a holy and righteous man, died in the thirty-third year of his reign when he sixty-three years old.

What a great change had taken place in Alma II: from sin and iniquity to chief judge and High Priest! This change is what happens when a person is born again of God. This is what belief and faith in the Lord Jesus Christ does. And when Jesus touches you, something happens – the love of God is shed abroad in your heart.

In the first year of the reign of the chief judge, there was a man brought before him to be judged, a man who was large, and noted for his great strength. He went among the people preaching to them what he termed to be the word of God, bearing down against the church, declaring to the people that every priest and teacher should be *popular* in their preaching. He believed that this popularity came from preaching what the people wanted to hear. He also taught that priests and teachers should not support themselves, but the people should support them.

This man, whose name was Nehor, also testified that all mankind would be saved at the last day, and that no one needed fear God's judgment. He tried to reason that the Lord created all men and in the end, he would save all people. Now many of the Nephites believed Nehor's teachings. They began to support him and give him money. His pride grew and grew and he soon began to wear very expensive clothing. He even started a church based on his new personal doctrine.

As Nehor went around the land preaching, he met a man that belonged to the church of God, an old man who was a teacher of the word of God and who had served God in many capacities throughout his life. This old man, whose name was Gideon, stood up to Nehor and challenged him with the true word of God. When he did so, Nehor took out a sword and killed Gideon, who was too old to defend himself. The people of the church took Nehor to the chief judge to be judged for the crime he had committed. Although he had committed a crime, he boldly stood before the chief judge proclaiming his doctrine. But Alma II, the chief judge, said to him,

> Behold, this is the first time that *priest craft* has been introduced among this people. You are not only guilty of priest craft but you endeavored to enforce it by the sword. And you have shed the blood of a righteous man. Therefore you are condemned to die according to the law.

Priest craft is the term used by God when people preach their own doctrine and set themselves up as a religious light to the world, but they do it that they may get gain and the praise of the world – they do not seek the welfare of Zion or to perform the work of the Lord. It appeals to the baser motives of men and women, who love the vain things of the world, as well as earthly riches, fame and honor.

They took Nehor and carried him to the top of a hill where he confessed, between the heavens and the earth, that his preaching was contrary to the word of God; and he suffered an ignominious death. Unfortunately, like many things when they are started, his confession and death did not put an end to the practice of priest craft.

Of course, people who practiced priest craft did not lie or bear false witness for fear of the law as the law did not stop a man from preaching what he claimed was his personal belief. Therefore, they *pretended* to preach according to their belief. They did not dare to steal, rob or murder for fear of the law; for these crimes, like lying, were punishable, including death for the person who murdered.

Now the people who did not belong to the church of God began to persecute those who did. The people of God were humble and not proud, and imparted the word of God without money and without price, as taught by God. This time became a great trial to those who stood fast in the faith, immovable in keeping the commandments of God.

The true and faithful ministers of God received no compensation when they ministered, preached, and taught the Word of God to the people. The people also took time away from their daily labors to hear the Word of God. And when they all heard the Word of God, they diligently returned to their jobs and labors. The preacher did not esteem himself above the hearer, nor the teacher above the learner; thus, they were all equal, and all labored according to their strength and ability. As well, they imparted their substance, every man according to that which he had to the poor, needy, sick, and afflicted. They did not wear expensive or fancy clothes, but they were neat, clean, and comely. Despite the persecution by those who didn't belong to the church, the Nephites and Lamanites had a time of peace.

In just a few years, wickedness and pride began infiltrating the church and there was much contention within it. This condition brought on the displeasure of God and usually great wars with the Lamanites. (As it turns out, these cycles of peace and war continued through decades and centuries. It was especially true when the majority of the people became sinful and transgressors of God's commandments.)

The chief judge and High Priest, Alma II, called on the people to repent, saying,

> Behold, my brethren of the church, have you spiritually been born of God? Have you received his image in your countenances? Have you experienced the mighty change in your hearts? Do you exercise faith in the redemption of Him who created you? Do you look forward with an eye of faith, and view this mortal body raised in immortality, and this corruption raised in incorruption, to stand before God to be judged according to the deeds, which have been done in the mortal body?

> Can you imagine to yourselves that in hearing the voice of the Lord saying unto you in that day: 'come unto me ye blessed, for behold, your works have been the works of righteousness upon the face of the earth.' Or do you imagine to yourselves that you can lie unto the Lord in that day, and

say, 'Lord, our works have been righteous works upon the face of the earth,' and that He will save you.

Or otherwise, can you imagine yourselves brought before the tribunal of God with your souls filled with guilt and remorse, having a remembrance of all your guilt, yes, a perfect remembrance of all your wickedness, yea, a remembrance that ye have set at defiance the commandments of God?

And I say unto you, you will know at that day you cannot be saved; for no man can be saved except his garments are washed white; his garments must be purified until they are cleansed from all stain, through the blood of him who was spoken by the prophets to redeem His people from their sins. Being guilty of all manner of wickedness, do you suppose such a one can have a place to sit down in the Kingdom of God, with Abraham, Isaac, Jacob, the holy prophets, and the Saints of God? I say unto you no, unless you make our creator a liar. And the scriptures say God cannot lie. So I say unto you, do away with pride, abominations, secret combinations, murder, and divers wickedness. For the Lord sends an invitation to all men, for the arms of mercy are extended toward them, saying, 'Come unto me and partake of the fruit of the tree of life, and you shall eat and drink of the bread and waters of life freely.'

As I previously mentioned, the Nephites were very industrious. They built many buildings and temples and even great cities, and as long as they served the Lord, they had peace and prosperity. All of this is reflected in the discoveries made of hidden cities, highways, and temples, pyramids and other types of buildings in Central and South America. All of it indicates that a great civilization once existed in America. It has been said that the Native Americans discovered by early Europeans were more *inheritors* than *creators* of the great buildings and cities.

About 82 BC a man by the name of Amulek, was on a journey to see a relative and an angel of the Lord appeared to him and said, "Amulek, return to your own house, for you shall feed a prophet of the Lord, a holy man, who is a chosen man of God; for he has fasted many days for the sins of this people and he is hungry. You shall receive him into your house and feed him, he shall call a blessing to you and your house." The man Amulek was told about was Alma II.

Later, Amulek testified to a crowd, "I obeyed the voice of the angel and returned to my house and found the holy man of God. He then lived with me for some time, teaching and exhorting the word of the Lord unto me. Learning the great plan of salvation, I then began to preach along with him the coming of our Lord and Savior, Jesus Christ, endeavoring to turn men and women from their sins and receive the word of the Lord, many times suffering persecution."

Not long after the above time, the four sons of King Mosiah, who had refused the kingship, had gone to the Lamanites to preach the word of God, and having faced many hardships, sufferings, and persecutions, returned to their homeland with their converts. God greatly blessed them during their fourteen-year missionary endeavor. As I previously mentioned, the Lamanites had lost all knowledge of the Lord and lived according to their own false traditions. They had a hatred of their brethren the Nephites. The four men, along with their missionary friends achieved great success converting many of the Lamanites.

These converted Indians possessed the wonderful love of God so much so that they forever refused to take up arms and fight anymore. Their desire was to shed no more blood, and as a symbol of this desire they buried all their weapons of war in the earth.

When their fellow Lamanites learned of their conversion, they came against them. But the converted ones went out to meet them and prostrated themselves on the earth, calling on the name of the Lord. They were in this position when their brethren began to slay them with the sword. And thus, without meeting any resistance, the unconverted Lamanites killed a thousand and five of their converted brethren, who died praising God. Now when their brethren saw this they stopped killing them and there were many whose hearts were filled with compassion and were converted. It turned out that the number converted was greater than the number killed. And by coming to the Lord, their darkness of skin was removed, and they became a fair and delightsome people. What a wonderful account of how the work of a few dedicated men among a hard hearted and evil people could make such an immense difference.

In the nineteenth year of the reign of judges, the High Priest, Alma II (he had resigned from the Chief Judge position to devote himself entirely to the work of God), came to his son, Helaman, and said to him,

> Believest thou the words which I spoke unto you concerning those records which I have kept? And Helaman said, Yes, I believe. Do you believe in Jesus Christ, who shall come? Yes, I believe in all the words you have spoken. Will you keep my commandments or the commandments of God? And he answered, Yes, I will keep thy commandments with all my heart. And his father said, Blessed art thou; and the Lord shall prosper thee in this land.

Then the High Priest and prophet of the Lord prophesied by the revelation of God that his people, the Nephites, would become extinct around AD 400 because of their sin and transgression, thus leaving the Lamanites sole possessors of this land (America). Alma II then turned over the gold plates or records containing the history and dealings of God and their great civilization here in America to his son.

The commandment of the Lord was to hand down these records from one generation to another to responsible men of God, until the extinction of this people. (The revelation came to pass when in AD 421 the last surviving prophet buried the abridged record in the earth.) Alma II then conferred the authority upon his son, left his homeland to go to another place, and was never heard of any more. His death and burial were unknown. He was a righteous man; and the saying went abroad throughout the church that he was taken up by the spirit, or buried by the hand of the Lord, even as Moses was.

Around 73 BC a man emerged from the Nephite people, with a cunning device and many flattering words. He was able to lead away the hearts of many people to live wickedly and to destroy the church of God, and to destroy the foundation of liberty that God granted unto them. A man by the name of Moroni, who was chief commander of the Nephite armies, heard of the dissension caused by this wicked man.

Moroni became angry, as the evil man enlisted the help of the Lamanites to overthrow the government of the people. Thus, a civil war was in the making. Moroni tore his coat; and he then took a piece of it, and wrote the following words on it: *"In memory of our God, our religion, and freedom, and our peace, our wives, and our children."* He then fastened the writing on the end of a pole (the writing was called the *Title of Liberty*).

After putting on his armor and helmet, Moroni bowed himself upon the earth, and he prayed mightily unto his God for the blessings of liberty to rest upon his brethren, so long as there should be a band of Christians remaining to possess the land, referring of course to all true believers in the coming of Christ as well as the true believers after the coming of Christ.

After he poured out his soul to God for a blessing upon this land, *a Chosen land, a Land of Liberty for the righteous*, he went among the people, waving the ripped part of his garment in the air, that all might see the writing which he had written upon it and crying with a loud voice, saying, "Behold, whosoever will maintain this Title upon the land, let them come forth in the strength of the Lord, and enter into a covenant that they will maintain their rights, and their religion, that the Lord God may bless them."

When Moroni proclaimed these words, the people came running together with their armor and they made a covenant (by tearing their garments), that they would not forsake the Lord their God; or in other words, if they should transgress the commandments of God or be ashamed to take upon them the name of Christ who was to come, that the Lord should destroy them even as they had torn their garments.

So they went out and fought for their land, religion, wives, and children, for their liberty, and for their freedom of worship of the true, living God. A great battle ensued against this wicked man, his followers, and the Lamanites. Many died, but the people of the Lord, whose faith and trust were in the Lord, were finally victorious in defending their rights.

Helaman, the son of Alma II, around 45 BC, conferred the authority and charge of the records to his son, Nephi (we will call him Nephi II). This was in the forty-eighth year of the judges. His father taught Nephi and brother Lehi, the ways of righteousness. They became great missionaries for the Lord, preaching the coming of Christ in the near future. They specifically prophesied that Jesus would be born of a Virgin in the land of their forefathers. They followed the example of the four sons of King Mosiah many years before and went among the Lamanites. Many believed in the words of these two righteous men and were converted. However, the devil was making inroads among their own people.

Preaching with the power of God, Nephi II exposed the Nephites abominations, iniquities, and transgressions. Nephi

II and Lehi warned the people by telling them that the judgments of God would soon come upon them. Some of his own people became angry with Nephi and influenced others to kill him. But the Lord was with him and said, "Behold, I will bless thee forever, I will make thee mighty in words and in deeds, and in faith and works, you shall have power to smite the earth." So, being obedient to the commandments of the Lord, he went among them and preached repentance. Unless they repented, the judgment of the Lord would come upon them.

Soon after this prophesy, around 20 BC, a great famine came upon the land. It came because Nephi had requested that God intervene and bring the people to repentance. As the famine wore on, many repented and became humble. So Nephi cried unto the Lord to send rain upon the land so that the famine would come to an end. And in the seventy-sixth year of the reign of judges the Lord turned away His anger and caused it to rain and the grain and fruits were harvested in their season. The people rejoiced and glorified God for his goodness. And they esteemed Nephi II as a great prophet having great power and authority. His brother Lehi was just like him.

Both the Lamanites and the Nephites lived in harmony and peace for a few years due to the preaching of the brothers and the power of God. But it was not long before the devil began to make inroads among both peoples. The devil caused a group of dissenters to emerge from the people. This group formed a band of robbers based on secret oaths. They plundered and murdered, and committed all sorts of crimes. They would hide in the mountains and wilderness where they could not be discovered except by those seeking to join them, which happened daily.

All of these events occurred in the eightieth year of the reign of judges. How sad to see that in a few years the devil blinded the hearts and minds of the people. They continued to the eighty-fifth year waxing deeper in pride and wickedness; thus they were ripening again for destruction. And you see that afflictions, famine, pestilence, war, and death are the result of wickedness and sin. Oh how foolish and how vain, evil, devilish, and quick to do iniquity, and how slow to do good, are the children of men! How quick they are to hearken to the words of the devil, and to set their hearts on the vain things of the world. An investigation of history will show that pride has often been the downfall of many nations and kingdoms.

In 6 BC a Lamanite by the name of Samuel came out of the converted Lamanites. He was called of God to be a prophet. He went into the land of the Nephites, where sin was abounding, to preach repentance. They took him and cast him out, and he was about to return to his own land, but the voice of the Lord came to him and said that he should return to the people and prophesy whatever should come into his heart. So he returned to the city and climbed upon a wall, cried with a loud voice the things that the Lord put in his heart.

> Destruction is coming to this people unless they repent. Have faith in the coming of the Lord Jesus Christ [in six years] for an angel of the Lord had declared this unto me, and he brought glad tidings to my soul and I was sent to bring glad tidings unto you.

> Behold, I give you a sign and this sign is that in five years the Son of God is to be born, to redeem all those who shall believe on His name. There shall be great lights in heaven in so much that in the night before he comes there shall be no darkness, and it shall appear unto man as if it was day. There shall be one day and a night and a day, as if it were one day, no night. For you shall know by the rising of the sun and by its setting that there were two days and a night. And another sign is that a new star shall arise that you have never beheld. Now this is not all, there shall be many signs and wonders in heaven and you shall be amazed, and wonder, that you shall fall to the earth. And whosoever believes on the Son of God shall have everlasting life. Thus, the Lord commanded me by the angel to tell you these things, and to command you to repent and prepare the way of the Lord.

> Here is another sign of His death. He surely must die [upon the cross] to bring to pass the resurrection of the dead, that men and women may be brought back into the presence of the Lord. He redeems all mankind from the first death – that spiritual death – for all mankind was cut off from the presence of the Lord because of the fall of Adam and are considered dead, both as to things temporal and to things spiritual. There is a physical death and there is a spiritual death.

I would like to explain the scriptures regarding flesh and spirit. This body of ours is composed of flesh, bone, blood, and a spirit (soul). The spirit is life. The physical death means the separation of the spirit from the body; the body returns to the mother earth, and the spirit (soul) returns to the God who gave it, to be temporarily judged. The spirit that God gives us never dies; it is eternal as God is eternal. The person who believes, repents, exercises faith, and dies in Christ, his soul goes to Paradise to wait for the morning of the First Resurrection.

The person who dies in sin, without Christ, his spirit goes to a place of darkness, where there shall be wailing, weeping, and gnashing of teeth, until the day of Resurrection. Resurrection is the reuniting of the spirit from Paradise to an incorruptible, immortal body, to dwell with Christ on earth for a thousand years (Satan will be bound, then loosed after the thousand years). The spirit in darkness will reunite with a body, to be condemned for eternity, banished from the presence of God to an everlasting punishment.

God is merciful, loving, and just. Foreseeing the fall of man who became sensual, devilish, and carnal, He provided a plan of redemption and salvation. Even though God is merciful He will not let mercy rob justice. This life is a probationary time and a preparatory state; thus He calls all people to have faith in Christ, to repent and be baptized for the remission of sins. Blessed is the man or woman who endures until the end.

Let's go back to Samuel. He continued prophesying to the Nephites, saying, "The Son of God shall be taken by wicked hands and put on the cross for the sins of the world." He also informed them concerning a great destruction to come upon this Western Hemisphere for the period of three hours during Christ's crucifixion when many shall die, and then three days of total darkness. (I will go into more detail on this a little later.)

There were some who believed the prophet, but many disbelieved and became angry with him. They began to cast stones at him and some shot arrows at him; but the power of God was with him, so much so that they could not hit him with the stones or the arrows. When they saw that they could not hit him, they said, "He has a devil." So they decided they needed to grab him. However, God allowed him to flee to his own land and began to preach and prophesy among his own people. He was never heard of any more among the Nephites.

As time passed, the inhabitants – both Nephites and Lamanites – became more wicked, with the exception of a few people of both nations. The prophet Nephi gave charge of all of the ancient records to his son, also named Nephi. The prophet departed from the land and was never heard of again. The son, receiving the power and authority from the Lord, began to preach repentance and baptism and informed the Nephites that the time was close when the birth of the Son of God would take place.

Some believed, but the majority disbelieved, persecuting the believers, saying, "Where is the sign that Samuel the Prophet spoke about on the city wall?" And they attempted to destroy the believers. The young prophet Nephi saw the situation and bowed down to earth in mighty prayer on behalf of his people. He cried all the day in mighty prayer; and then the voice of the Lord came unto him, saying,

> Lift up your head and be of good cheer; for the time is at hand, and on this night shall the sign be given, and on the morrow come I into the world, to show the world that I will fulfill all that which I have caused to be spoken by the mouth of my holy prophets, from the foundation of the world. This night shall the sign be given.

The words of Samuel were fulfilled; at sunset, there was no darkness. The people were astonished and fell to the earth with great fear. They knew that the prophets had testified of these things for many years, and that the sign, which had been given, came to pass. After what should have been the night, the sun rose in the morning according to its proper order. The people knew it was the day that the Lord should be born. A new star also appeared in the heavens, fulfilling the word of the Lord. The ninety-second year of the judges passed, and many signs and prophecies spoken by the holy prophets were fulfilled.

To help the reader focus on the time period, let's summarize it. It was six hundred and nine years since the Israelite colony left Jerusalem; one hundred years since the establishment of judges (and a form of democracy); and nine years passed since the signs were given concerning the birth of Christ. Now the Nephites changed their calendar to match the sign of the coming of Christ, so that they began to reckon their time from this period on, in other words it was now AD 9 for them.

In AD 13 there began to be wars and contentions throughout the whole land. A band of robbers that hid in the mountains became quite numerous. Dissenters from both the Nephites and the Lamanites joined up with them. They would raid cities, rob, murder, and destroy throughout the land, and would then flee into the mountains to hide. This caused the two nations to form a unified front against them. They were believers in Christ, yet they were compelled to take up arms for the safety of their lives, women, and children; also to maintain their rights, freedom, and liberty. The Lamanites who were converted and united with the Nephites lost their dark skin and became white like the people of God.

After subduing their common enemy, the two nations had a period of peace. The Nephites and the converted Lamanites began to prosper, during which time many cities and highways were built. But in a few years new disputes arose among the people. This occurrence was due to pride and boasting by some because of their exceeding great riches. There were many merchants, lawyers, and officers and the people began to be distinguished by ranks, according to their riches and their education. Some were ignorant because of their poverty, and others obtained great learning because of their riches. Some were humble, and did not return curses with curses, but rather they took the curses, persecution, and all manner of affliction with humility, and were penitent before God.

This inequality grew and expanded until even the members of the church were affected and the church began to deteriorate. Only a few Lamanites remained faithful and true to the word of God. They were strong in the faith, immovable, firm, and steadfast, diligently keeping the commandments of God. Behind the pride and greed was Satan. He encouraged them (or enticed them) to seek power, riches, and the vain things of the world. He wanted them to be more materialistic.

By AD 30 their state of wickedness was frightful. I would like to note that they did not sin ignorantly, for they knew the will of God, having been taught it by good and holy men. Therefore, they willfully rebelled against God. (At this same time in Galilee, Jesus Christ had begun his public ministry.)

Men inspired from heaven went among the people in all the land, preaching and testifying boldly of the sins and iniquities of the people. They also preached about the plan of redemption, the suffering, death, and resurrection of Christ. The lawyers, judges, priests, and those who loved the vain things of the world became very angry with those who testified against them. Evil men endeavored once again to set up a king and this event caused a division among the people. They banded together and formed what was called a secret combination (like organized crime or the 'mob'). Eventually they picked a man to be their king. This secret combination caused great havoc among the people. They committed crimes such as robbery and murder. It became so bad that only a few righteous people remained.

The prophet Nephi (a descendant of the first Nephi) went among the people and preached repentance and baptism for the remission of sins. Through the power of God he performed signs and miracles. He ministered to the believers with great power and authority. So great was his faith in the Lord Jesus Christ that angels ministered to him daily. In the name of Jesus, he cast out devils and unclean spirits and his brother, who had been stoned to death, he raised from the dead. Nephi also warned the wicked that in a matter of a few years, the signs of God's judgment (and destruction) would be fulfilled as foretold by the prophets. However, there were great doubts and disputations among the people concerning those signs and prophecies. As we shall see in the next chapter, the people paid a dear price for ignoring the prophecies and the signs and wonders.

Chapter Twelve

Jesus Christ In Ancient America

In AD 34 the time arrived for the fulfillment of the signs given by the holy prophets. The following is the account of what occurred in the land of America (as recorded in the Translated Ancient American Record):

And it came to pass in the thirty and fourth year, in the first month on the fourth day of the month, there arose a great storm, such as never had been known in all the land. And there was also a great and terrible tempest; and there was terrible thunder, insomuch that it did shake the whole earth as if it was about to divide asunder. And there was exceeding sharp lightning, such as never had been known in all the land. Cities were burned, coastal cities were sunk in the sea, and all its inhabitants were drowned. Some were buried in the earth, others were covered up by the earth. A great and terrible destruction occurred in the land southward [South America], but there was a greater destruction in the land northward [North America].

The whole face of the land was changed, because of the tempest, whirlwinds, thundering, lightning, and earth quakes; highways were broken up, level roads were spoiled, and smooth places became rough. A great many of the inhabitants were killed. Some were carried away by the whirlwind, and where they went no one knew. The whole face of the earth became deformed. Rocks were rent in twain, broken in fragments, in seams and cracks. [This is evident in America today.]

Now all of this was done in the space of about three hours. Then there was total darkness in all the land. The darkness was so thick that those not killed could feel the vapor of darkness. There could be no light from candles, torches, or kindled fire; no glimmer or light seen from the sun, stars or the moon. This darkness lasted for three days. The three hours of destruction in the Americas was during the time that Christ was on the cross. And the three days of dark- ness were during the time that Christ's body was in the tomb.

There was great mourning, howling, groaning, and weeping by those who were spared. They were heard to cry and mourn, saying, 'O that we had repented before this great and terrible day, and had not killed and stoned the prophets, and cast them out; then would our mothers and our fair daughters, our children, our fathers, sons, and the people be spared.'

After the third day of darkness, a voice was heard by those who were spared] saying, 'Woe, woe, woe, unto this people; woe unto the inhabitants of the whole earth except them who repent; for the devil laughs and his angels rejoice, because of the slain of the fair sons and daughters of my people; and it is because of their iniquity and abominations that they are fallen, that their cities and land were destroyed, and that the blood of the prophets and saints should not come up any more unto me against them.' And many other things did the voice say unto the people.

The voice that came from heaven continued to say,

Oh all of you who were spared because you were more righteous, will you now return unto me and repent of your sins, and be converted, that I may heal you? Yea, verily, I say unto you, if you will come unto me you shall have eternal life. Behold, mine arm of mercy is extended toward you and whosoever will come, him will I receive: and blessed are those who come unto me. Behold, I am Jesus Christ, the Son of God. I created the heavens and the earth, and all things that are in it. I was with the Father from the beginning, I am in the Father and the Father in me; and in me hath the Father glorified his name.

I came to my own, and my own received me not. And the scriptures concerning my coming are fulfilled. And as many as have received me, to them have I given to become the sons of God; and believe on my name, for behold, by me redemption cometh, and in me is the Law of Moses fulfilled. I am the light and the life of the world. I am Alpha and Omega, the beginning and the end. And ye shall offer up unto me no more the shedding of blood; yea, your sacrifices and your burnt offerings shall be done away, for I will accept none of your sacrifices and your burnt offerings. And you shall offer for a sacrifice unto me a broken heart and a contrite spirit. And whosoever comes to me with a broken heart and a contrite spirit, him will I baptize with fire and with the Holy Ghost. Behold, I have come into the world to bring redemption unto the world, to save the world from sin. Therefore, whosoever repents and comes unto me as a little child, him will I receive, for of such is the kingdom of God. Behold, for such have I lain down my life, and have taken it up again; therefore, repent, and come unto me ye ends of the earth, and be saved.

There was a great multitude of people gathered together round about the temple that was in the land called *Bountiful*; and they were marveling and wondering one with another, and were showing one to another the great and marvelous change that had taken place. And they were also conversing about this Jesus Christ, of whom the sign had been given concerning his death.

And while they were conversing one with another, they heard a voice as if it came out of heaven; and they cast their eyes round about, for they understood not the voice they heard; and it was not a harsh voice, neither was it a loud voice; nevertheless, being a small voice it did pierce them who did hear it to the center, insomuch that there was no part of their frame that it did not cause to quake; yea it did pierce them to the very soul, and did cause their hearts to burn.

Again they heard the voice, and they did not understand it. Again, for the third time, they heard the voice, hearing attentively, and turned their eyes steadfastly toward heaven from where the sound came. Now this time they understood the voice they heard; and it said unto them, "Behold, my Beloved Son, in whom I am well-pleased, in whom I have glorified my name -hear ye him." And as they looked toward heaven, they saw a man descending out of heaven; and He was clothed in a white robe; and he came down and stood in the midst of them.

The eyes of the whole multitude were turned upon him, and they durst not open their mouths, even one to another, and knowing not what it meant, for they thought it was an angel that had appeared unto them. He stretched forth His hand and spoke unto the people, saying, "Behold, I am Jesus Christ, whom the prophets testified shall come into the world. I am the light and the life of the world; and I have drunk out of that bitter cup which the Father had given me, and have glorified the Father in taking upon me the sins of the world, in which I have suffered the will of the Father in all things from the beginning."

And when Jesus had spoken these words, the whole multitude fell to the earth; for they remembered that it had been prophesied among them that Christ should show himself unto them after his ascension into heaven. And He said unto them, "Arise and come forth unto me, that you may thrust your hands into my side, and also that you may feel the prints of the nails in my hands and in my feet, that you may know that I am the God of Israel, and the God of the whole earth, and have been slain for the sins of the world."

The multitude went forth, and thrust their hands into His side, and did feel the prints of the nails in His hands and in His feet; this they did, going forth one by one until they had all gone forth, and did see with their eyes and did feel with their hands, and know of a surety, and bore record it was He of whom it was written by the prophets that He should come. And they all went forth and witnessed for themselves, cried out in one accord, saying, "Hosanna! Blessed be the name of the Most High God." And they fell down at the feet of Jesus and worshipped Him.

He spoke to the prophet Nephi, for he was among the multitude, and the Lord commanded him to come forth. And he went forth and bowed himself before the Lord and kissed his feet. The Lord commanded him to arise and he arose, stood before Him, and the Lord said to him, "I give unto you power that you shall baptize this people when I am again ascended into heaven." And He called others, and said unto them likewise, giving them power to baptize, informing them, "On this wise shall you baptize, there shall be no disputations among you. Verily I say unto you, that who so repents of his sins through your words and desires to be baptized in my name, on this wise shall you baptize them- behold, you shall go down and stand in the water, and in my name shall you baptize them. And now these are the words you shall say, calling them by name, saying, 'Having authority given me of Jesus Christ, I baptize you in the name of the Father, and of the Son, and of the Holy Ghost. Amen.' And then shall you immerse them in the water, and come forth again out of the water. After this manner shall you baptize in my name; for behold, verily I say unto you that the Father, and the Son, and the Holy Ghost are one.

And according as I have commanded you, thus shall you baptize. And there shall be no disputations among you, as there have been; neither shall there be disputations among you concerning the points of my doctrine, as there have hitherto been. For verily, verily I say unto you, he who has the spirit of contention is not of me, but is of the devil, who is the father of contention, and he stirs up the hearts of men to contend with anger, one with another. Behold, this is not my doctrine, to stir up the hearts of men with anger, one against another; but this is my doctrine that such things should be done away. And this is my doctrine, and it is the doctrine which the Father had given unto me; and I bear record of the Father, and the Holy Ghost bears record of the Father and me; and I bear record that the Father commands all men, everywhere, to repent and believe in me. And who so believes in me, and is baptized, the same shall be saved; and they are they who shall inherit the kingdom of God. Who so believes not in me, and is not baptized, shall be damned.

Verily, verily, I say unto you, that this is my doctrine, and I bear record of it from the Father; and whoso believes in me believes in the Father also; and unto him will the Father bear record of me, for He will visit him with fire and with the Holy Ghost. And thus will the Father bear record of me, and the Holy Ghost will bear record unto him of the Father and me; for the Father, and I, and the Holy Ghost, are one.

Again I say unto you, you must repent, and become as a little child, and be baptized in my name, or you can in nowise receive these things. And again I say unto you, you must repent, and be baptized in my name, and become as a little child, or you can in nowise inherit the kingdom of God. Verily, verily, I say unto you, that this is my doctrine, and who so builds upon this builds upon my rock, and the gates of hell shall not prevail against them. And who so shall declare more or less than this – and establish it for my doctrine – the same comes of evil, and is not built upon my rock; but he builds upon a sandy foundation, and the gates of hell stand open to receive such when the floods come and the winds beat upon them. Therefore, go forth unto this people, and declare the words which I have spoken, unto the ends of the earth.

Now when Jesus had spoken these words to the prophet and to the ones he had called, the number of them were twelve, receiving the power and authority to baptize. He stretched forth his hand unto the multitude, and cried unto them, saying, "Blessed are you if you shall give heed unto the words of these twelve whom I have chosen from among you to minister unto you, and to be your servants; and unto them I have given power that they may baptize you with water; and after you are baptized with water, behold, I will baptize you with fire and with the Holy Ghost; therefore, blessed are you if you shall believe in me and be baptized after that, you have seen me and know that I am.

And again, more blessed are they who shall testify that you have seen me and that you know that I am. Yea, blessed are they who shall believe in your words, and come down into the depths of humility and be baptized, for they shall be visited with fire and with the Holy Ghost, and shall receive a remission of their sins."

How glorious was Jesus' appearance to the people of this land (America)! We have heard from various tribes of Indians in America that a white-personage with a beard once walked the Americas, performed many miracles and signs, and predicted their restoration. However, before their restoration takes place, the United States and the other gentile nations in America will be judged, because of their iniquities and sin. The wicked must perish and the righteous, few though they may be, shall be spared. It is evident that the gentile nations of America are heading for a fall. Great nations and empires have fallen because of their internal corruption. Theologians, statesmen, and even the common person have stated it. All have perceived the terrible situation these nations and the world are in today.

The Savior repeated to the Nephites and Lamanites gathered in the Land Bountiful the *Sermon on the Mount*, which He taught His followers in Galilee, with little variation. And they marveled at the teachings of Jesus. He called twelve men to be His special witnesses, ordained them with power and authority just as he ordained the twelve in Judea. (In America He called these twelve men *Disciples*, but in the land of Judea he called the twelve he had chosen *Apostles*.)

Jesus informed them that they were the other sheep that He referred to when He spoke to His followers in Judea (see John 10:16). He explained in Judea that the other sheep, in other lands, must hear His voice so that there would be one fold and one shepherd.

He continued teaching the people in Ancient America, as recorded in the following passage:

He looked upon the people and said unto them, "Behold, my time is at hand (to go to the Father and return on the morrow). I perceive that ye are weak, that you cannot understand all my words, which I am commanded of the Father to speak unto you at this time. Therefore, go ye unto your homes, and ponder upon the things, which I have said, and ask the Father, in my name, that you may understand, and prepare your minds for the morrow, and I come unto you again. But now I go unto the Father and also to show myself unto the lost tribes of Israel, for they are not lost unto the Father, for He knows whither He has taken them."

When Jesus had spoken thus, He cast His eyes round about again on the people, and beheld that they were in tears. They looked steadfastly upon Him as if they would ask Him to tarry a little longer with them. And He said unto them, "Behold, my bowels are filled with compassion toward you. Have you any that are sick among you? Bring them hither. Have you any that are lame, blind, halt, maimed, leprous, withered, deaf, or afflicted in any manner? Bring them here and I will heal them, for I have compassion upon you; my bowels are filled with mercy. For I perceive that you desire that I should show unto you what I have done unto your brethren at Jerusalem, for I see that your faith is sufficient that I should heal you." And they brought to Him all who were in need, and He healed every one of them. And they all bowed down at His feet and worshipped Him. And many did kiss His feet insomuch that they bathed His feet with their tears.

And He commanded that their little children be brought, and Jesus stood in the midst. He commanded the people to kneel on the ground. And when they knelt upon the ground, Jesus groaned within himself, and said, "Father, I am troubled because of the wickedness of the people of the house of Israel." When He had said these words, He himself also knelt upon the earth; and behold, he prayed unto the Father, and the things which he prayed cannot be written and the multitude bore record who heard Him. The eye had never seen, neither had the ear heard before, so great and marvelous things as they saw and heard Jesus speak unto the Father; and no tongue can speak nor can there be written by any man, neither can the hearts of men conceive so great and marvelous things as were both seen and heard; and no one can conceive of the joy which filled their souls at the time they heard Him pray for them unto the Father.

What an experience these people had witnessed – to see and hear the wonderful prayer of our Lord. Righteous men before and after Christ desired to have such a testimony. How wonderful it would have been to be present at the time of His appearance in America after His resurrection, or in the land of Judea when He walked the earth, teaching the great things of the kingdom of God. However, by belief and faith in Christ we have joy and happiness through the power of the Holy Ghost. We know that these things are true. Hosanna, unto the Lord and glory to God in the highest. Let us continue with the record.

Jesus had made an end of praying unto the Father. He arose; but so great was the joy of the multitude that they were overcome, and He spoke unto them, and commanded them to arise. And they arose from the earth, and He said unto them, "Blessed are you because of your faith, and now behold, my joy is full." And when He had said these words, He wept, and the multitude observed. He took their little children, one by one, and blessed them, and prayed unto the Father for them, and when He had done this, He wept again. And He said unto them, "Behold, your little ones."

And as they looked, then cast their eyes heavenward, the heavens opened and angels, descending out of heaven as it were in the midst of fire, encircled those little ones about, and they were encircled about with fire; and the angels ministered unto them. Now they knew that this great and miraculous event was true, for they witnessed it for themselves.

Jesus commanded the twelve disciples He had chosen to get some bread and wine and bring it to Him. While they were gone, He commanded the people to sit down upon the earth. When they returned with the bread and wine, He took bread and broke and blessed it and commanded His disciples to eat and distribute it among the people. "You will receive power to do this among my people of the church, unto those who shall believe and be baptized in my name. You shall do this in remembrance of my body, which I have shown unto you. And it shall be a testimony unto the Father that ye do always remember me and ye shall have my Spirit to be with you."

He then commanded His disciples to take the cup of wine and drink of it, and to give also to the people to drink of it, and they were filled. And when the disciples had done this,

Jesus said unto them, "Blessed are you for this thing which you have done, for this is fulfilling my commandments, and this does witness unto the Father that you are willing to do that which I have commanded you. Ye shall do it in remembrance of my blood, which I have shed for you that you may witness unto the Father that you always remember me and you shall have my spirit to be with you always."

Now Jesus taught them many other things and then He informed them that He must go to the Father and would return on the morrow. A cloud came down and overshadowed them that they could not see Jesus, and while they were overshadowed, He departed from them, and ascended into heaven. And the disciples saw and bore record that He ascended into heaven.

(I would like to note that in Jerusalem, Jesus met with his disciples for the Passover meal and he instituted a new doctrine when he took bread, blessed it and broke it and gave it to his disciples and said, "Take, eat; this is my body." And He took the cup filled with wine, and gave thanks, and gave it to them, saying, "Drink ye all of it; for this is my blood of the New Testament, which is shed for many for the remission of sins. These do in remembrance of me." Thus was the communion or Lord's Supper instituted in the church of Jesus Christ.)

There were about two thousand and five hundred people who witnessed the above miracles and blessings. They bore testimony of all the things they saw and heard. Now, after Jesus ascended into heaven, the people dispersed, and returned to their respective homes. Immediately people told their relatives, friends, and neighbors about all that happened. How they saw Jesus, and how He ministered to them. They also explained how Jesus would return the next morning. Many people traveled all night that they might be where Jesus would show Himself in the morning.

So the next day the people gathered together, with the prophet Nephi and the other eleven disciples organizing them. These twelve men also went among the people, instructing them to separate into twelve bodies. And the twelve disciples did teach them the commandments of Jesus, and caused them to kneel again upon the earth, and to pray unto the Father in the name of Jesus. After teaching the people, the disciples again knelt upon the earth to pray unto the Father in the name of Jesus. And they prayed that the Holy Ghost be given unto them. After praying, they went down to the water's edge. The prophet went down into the water and was baptized, then he baptized the eleven and when they all came out of the water, they were filled with the Holy Ghost and with fire. And the fire that came down from heaven encircled them about and the people did witness and bear record of it.

Angels then came down from heaven and ministered unto the disciples and Jesus also appeared in the midst of them and ministered to them. Afterwards, Jesus separated himself from the people and bowed Himself upon the earth and uttered a great and beautiful prayer in behalf of His disciples and those that would hear and keep His commandments.

Jesus miraculously provided bread and wine, blessed it, and gave it to His disciples and commanded them to eat and drink. They then gave to the people, in remembrance of the great and eternal sacrifice Jesus made for them and for all who will obey. And He said unto them, "He that eats this bread eats of my body to his soul; and he that drinks of this wine drinks of my blood to his soul; and his soul shall never hunger nor thirst, but shall be filled." After they had participated in the communion, they were filled with the spirit of God, and they cried out with one voice, giving glory to Jesus, whom they both saw and heard.

Jesus explained to the people about their future and that of the tribes of Israel scattered throughout the world. He continued, saying,

> Verily, verily, I say unto you the time will come for the fulfilling of the covenants, which the Father had made unto His people. 0 House of Israel, then shall the remnants be gathered in from the east, west, south, and north, and shall be brought to the knowledge of the Lord their God, who had redeemed them.

> The Father commanded me that I should give unto you [Native Americans] this land for your inheritance. And if the gentiles [Americans] do not repent after the blessing they have received in this land [America] and have scattered my people [Native Americans] and taken their land, then shall you who are a remnant of the house of Jacob [Native Americans] go forth among them, [Americans] and be in the midst of them [Americans], who shall be many. And you shall be among them as a lion among the beasts of the forest, and as a young lion among the flocks of sheep, who, if he goes

through, both treads down and tears in pieces, and none can deliver. And I will gather my people together as a man gathers his sheaves into the floor. And it shall come to pass that I will establish my people, 0 House of Israel.

Here Jesus prophesied concerning the remnants of Jacob, who are the descendants of his son Joseph (Native Americans), saying they shall be among the Americans like a lion among the beast of the forest, and a young lion among the sheep. Could this possibly refer to militant Indians? Generally, a young lion will kill indiscriminately, whereas an older lion will only kill for food. This may indicate the possible violence against, not all people, but those who resist the will and message of God, and thus become prey.

The Native Americans must unite as a people, a nation, and abandon the old traditions, customs, idolatry, and sin and become a righteous people, with unity of purpose. A leader will emerge from among them, a righteous and holy man. He will be like Moses, a Deliverer, so that he will be an American Indian Moses. (He will also be a Seer and we will go into more detail concerning him a little later.) Until that day, militant Native Americans may emerge and cause disturbances throughout the land. The Lord does not condone violence, destruction, terrorism, crime, or sin in any degree. The establishment of the American Indian to the land of their inheritance (America) shall be achieved through righteousness and the acceptance of Jesus, who once walked the Americas among their ancestors.

Jesus in His predictions informs us that the Americans were to be established in this land as a free people by the power of God. For how long depends on their spiritual status. It is apparent that the situation in America is getting worse, and the spiritual status is declining. The increase in violence, crime, materialism, and sin is also evident. Not only in America, but the entire world. How long will God tolerate it? Until sin becomes ripened, then His judgment strikes.

Jesus continues the predictions saying,

Woe be unto the gentiles except those who repent and are baptized for the remission of sins, for it shall come to pass in that day, saith the Father, that I will cut off thy horses out of the midst of thee, and I will destroy thy chariots (means of transportation and instruments of war). I will cut off the cities of thy land, and throw down all thy strongholds. And I will cut off witchcraft, and there shall be no more soothsayers. The graven images I will also cut off, and thy standing images out of the midst of thee, and you shall no more worship the works of thy hands. And I will pluck up thy groves out of the midst of thee; so will I destroy thy cities. And it shall come to pass that all lyings, deceivings, envyings, strifes, priest crafts, and whoredoms shall be done away.

Here we see that Jesus foretells the situation in America and what is going to happen in the land someday. In the next chapter we learn more about the future of America.

Chapter Thirteen

A New Native American City Foretold

After Jesus made His second appearance among the Nephites and Lamanites and performed many signs and miracles, as well as miraculously providing bread and wine for the people in remembrance of His eternal sacrifice, He then began again to exhort and expound the scriptures and made predictions concerning a holy city in America. Here they are: (Also see the next chapter concerning the restoration of the Native Americans.)

For it shall come to pass, saith the Father, that at that day whosoever will not repent and come unto my Beloved Son, them will I cut off from among my people, 0 House of Israel. And I will execute vengeance and fury upon them, even as upon the heathen, such as they have not heard. But if they will repent and hearken unto my words, and harden not their hearts, I will establish my church among them, and they shall come in unto the covenant and be numbered among this the remnant of Jacob [righteous Lamanites] unto whom I have given this land for their inheritance; and they [gentiles] shall assist my people, the remnant of Jacob, and also as many of the house of Israel [Jews] shall come, that they may build a city, which shall be called the *NEW JERUSALEM*. And they shall assist in gathering in all who are scattered upon the face of the land, in unto the *New Jerusalem*. [Emphasis added by author.]

And then shall the power of heaven come down among them; and I also will be in their midst. And then shall the work of the Father commence at that day, even when this gospel shall be preached among the Lamanites. Verily I say unto you, at that day shall the work of the Father commence among all the dispersed of my people, yea, even the tribes which have been lost, which the Father had led away out of Jerusalem. And prepare the way whereby they may call on the Father in my name. Then shall the work commence, with the Father, among all nations, in preparing the way that His people may be gathered home to the land of their inheritance. And they shall go out from all nations; and they shall not go out in haste, nor go by flight, for I will go before them, saith the Father, and I will be their rearward.

According to the revelations of God, this Western Hemisphere is going to be a land for the righteous, a government of God for the righteous, and this nation, under God, shall have a new birth. A government of God, by the people of God, for the people of God, shall not perish from the earth. It shall be a godly government, whose President shall be the King of Kings, the Lord Jesus Christ. This land has been designated to be the headquarters of the Church of Jesus Christ.

The descendants of Ephraim and Manasseh (sons of Joseph) and the converted Jews and gentiles of this land will create a great, holy nation. This government of God (Zion) shall be established while in the flesh or blood life, not after the Resurrection. There shall be a peaceful reign for many years, while in other parts of the world the nations shall be in distress, confusion, pestilence, hunger, and war. Many shall attempt to come to this land. And the Lord shall send out Godly fishers into the world for the last time to bring salvation unto them. Then the restoration of the House of Israel shall take place and Jerusalem will again become the holy city of the Lord.

This holy city, the *NEW JERUSALEM,* and the *PEACEFUL REIGN* in America (Zion), are described by the prophet Isaiah:

And there shall come forth a rod out of the stem of Jesse [Jesus Christ] and a branch shall grow out of his roots: And the spirit of the Lord shall rest upon Him, the spirit of wisdom and understanding, the spirit of counsel and might, the spirit of knowledge and of the fear of the Lord; and shall make Him of quick understanding in the fear of the Lord; and He shall not judge after the sight of His eyes, neither reprove after the hearing of his ears. For with righteousness shall He judge the poor, and reprove with equity for the meek of the earth; and He shall smite the earth with the rod of His mouth, and with the breath of His lips shall He slay the wicked [the cleansing of America]. And righteousness shall be the girdle of his loins, and faithfulness the girdle of His reigns.

The wolf also shall dwell with the lamb, and the leopard shall lie down with the kid; and the calf and young lion and the fatling together; and a little child shall lead them. And the cow and the bear shall feed; their young ones shall lie down together; and the lion shall eat straw like the ox. And the suckling child shall play on the hole of the asp, and the weaned child shall put his hand on the cockatrice den. They shall not hurt or destroy in all my holy mountain; for the earth shall be full of the knowledge of the Lord [never in the history of the world have we had the means to print, publish, or broadcast salvation to the world] as the waters cover the sea.

And in that day there shall be a root of Jesse [Jesus Christ, and His Church] which shall stand for an ensign to the people; to it shall the gentiles seek: and his rest shall be glorious. And it shall come to pass in that day that the Lord shall set His hand again the second time to recover the remnant of His people [House of Israel]. [However, before the restoration of the house of Israel takes place, the time of the gentiles must be completed. The establishment of Israel since 1948 is simply a prelude until God takes a direct hand in the matter.]

And He shall set up an ensign [Jesus Christ and His church] for the nations, and shall assemble the outcasts of Israel [ten lost tribes] and gather together the dispersed of Judah [Jews] from the four corners of the earth. The envy also of Ephraim shall depart, and the adversaries of Judah shall be cut off, Ephraim shall not envy Judah, and Judah shall not vex Ephraim. But they shall fly upon the shoulders of the Philistines toward the west; they shall spoil them of the east together; they shall lay their hand upon Edom and Moab; and the children of Ammon shall obey them.

And the Lord shall utterly destroy the tongue of the Egyptian sea; and with His mighty wind shall He shake His hand over the river, and shall smite it in seven streams, and make men go over dry-shod. And there shall be a highway for the remnant of His people, which shall be left, from Assyria like as it was to Israel in the day that he came up out of the land of Egypt.

Please refer to the prophet Jeremiah, chapter 23, one of the many verses concerning the restoration of the house of Israel, or its remnants: "Therefore, behold, the days come, saith the Lord, that they shall no more say 'the Lord lives which brought up the children of Israel out of the land of Egypt,' but, 'the Lord lives which brought up and which led the seed of the house of Israel out of the north country and from all countries whither I have driven them; and they shall dwell in their own land.'"

In the closing chapter of the prophet Amos, we have a prophecy which cannot be misunderstood: "And I will bring again the captivity of my people of Israel, and they shall build the waste cities, and inhabit them; and they shall plant vineyards and drink the wine thereof; and they shall also make gardens, and eat the fruit of them. And I will plant them upon their land, and they shall no more be pulled up out of their land which I have given them, saith the Lord, your God."

There are other prophecies by many prophets foretelling the restoration of the house of Israel to the land of its inheritance (Lamanites to America and other tribes of Israel to Judea-Palestine or other lands of inheritance). This restoration shall be accomplished soon, but not until after much tribulation and suffering. After the period of great peace (which we previously called the *Peaceful Reign*), Jesus Christ returns to begin the millennium (1,000 years) with His Saints upon the earth. The wicked shall be reserved for judgment, the righteous saved, and the earth shall be cleansed to be used as the abiding place of the saints of the most high God.

In the meantime the dragon, that old serpent which is the Devil, shall be bound for the thousand years. And those who suffered persecution and death in diverse ways, the spirits of them and the righteous shall be resurrected at the return of Christ, live and reign with Him for the thousand years. But the rest of the dead will not again until the thousand years are expired. This is the *First Resurrection.* As the Scriptures say, 'Blessed and holy is he that has part in the First Resurrection; on such the second death hath no power, but they shall be priests of God and of Christ, and shall reign with Him for the thousand years.' After the thousand years, Satan shall be loosed out of prison for a short season. He shall go out to deceive the nations which are in the four quarters of the earth, Gog and Magog, to gather them together to battle: the number of whom is as the sands of the sea.

This little season that Satan will be loosed will be for the last time. He will endeavor to bring as many souls as he can down to hell with him. He will gather the deceived together to give battle to the people of God. The Apostle John (or John the Revelator) in the *Book of Revelation,* twentieth chapter, says that Satan and his army,

...went up on the breadth of the earth, and compassed the camp of the Saints about, and the beloved city: and fire came from God out of Heaven, and devoured them. And the Devil that deceived them was cast into the lake of fire and brimstone, where the beast and the false prophet are, and shall be tormented day and night forever and ever. And I saw a great white throne, and him that sat on it, from whose face the earth and the heaven fled away; and there was found no place for them.

And I saw the dead, small and great, stand before God; and the books were opened: and another book was opened, which is the book of life: and the dead were judged out of those things which were written in the books, according to their works. And the sea gave up the dead that were in it; and death and hell delivered up the dead which were in them; and they were judged every man according to their works. And death and hell were cast into the lake of fire. This is the second death. And whosoever was not found written in the book of life was cast into the lake of fire.

Let us go back to the Translated Ancient Nephite Records and the time Jesus was among the people here. For three days He taught the people many things, quoting the prophets and explaining the Scriptures, healing the sick, the lame, opening the eyes of the blind and the ears of the deaf. He even raised a man from the dead. The people heard their children, and even babes, utter marvelous things.

Jesus ascended back to the Father, but returned often among the people. The twelve disciples whom Jesus had chosen began to preach and baptize, and to teach as many as were converted. All those who were baptized in the name of Jesus were filled with the Holy Ghost. As in Jerusalem after the ascension of Jesus, the members of His church had all things in common, every man dealing justly with one another. (Having all things in common was the result of the love of God that was in their hearts.) And most importantly, they did all the things Jesus commanded that they should do. Those who were baptized were called the Church of Jesus Christ.

I would like to point out that the disciples of Jesus in Ancient America were confused about the name of the church. While they were in prayer Jesus appeared to them and said, "And how be it my church save it be called in my name? For if a church be called in Moses name then it be Moses' church; or if it be called in the name of a man then it be the church of a man; but if it be called in my name then it is my church, if so be that they are built upon my gospel."

Before Jesus' final ascension to heaven, He gathered His disciples, "What is it ye desire of me after I am gone to the Father?" And they all spoke, with the exception of three, and said, "We desire that after we have lived unto the age of man, and our ministry in which you have called us has an end, that we may speedily come unto thee in thy kingdom." And He said unto them, "Blessed are ye because ye desired this thing of me; therefore, after that ye are seventy-two years old ye shall come unto me in my kingdom; and with me ye shall find rest."

Here Jesus has promised them, the nine disciples, that when they reach the age of seventy-two, their spirit shall go to Paradise or the kingdom of the Lord. Their bodies shall return to the mother earth to wait the morning of the First Resurrection, at the return of Jesus.

After He had spoken to the nine, He turned to the remaining three, and said to them, "What will ye that I should do unto you, when I am gone unto the Father?" And they sorrowed in their hearts, for they dared not speak unto Him the thing, which they desired. And He said unto them, "Behold, I know your thoughts, and ye have desired the thing which John [the Apostle in Jerusalem and brother of James] my beloved, who was with me in my ministry, before I was lifted up [on the cross] desired of me."

It was traditionally assumed that the Apostle John died about AD 100, however, Jesus tells us in the scriptures that John never died. Let us go to the Bible and see what is recorded concerning John, Chapter 21. After Jesus' resurrection, he appeared to His Apostles while they were fishing, making it the third time He appeared to them, He called them from the shore and said, "Come and dine" and they went. The Lord asked Peter three times if he loved him and Peter answered Him every time, "You know that I love you." And Jesus said to him, 'Feed my lambs and feed my sheep.' John was following, and Peter said to Jesus, "Lord, and what shall this man do?" Jesus responded, "If I will that he tarry until I come, does that matter to you? Follow me." After that comment, the word went among the saints that John would not die. Of course, Jesus did not specifically say that to him, but distinctly implied it.

So Jesus then told the Three Disciples,

More blessed are you, for you shall never taste of death; but
you shall live to behold all the things of the Father unto the
children of men, even until all things shall be fulfilled
according to the will of the Father, when I shall come in my
glory with the powers of heaven. And ye shall never endure
the pains of death; but when I shall come in my glory, ye
shall be changed in the twinkling of an eye from mortality to
immortality; and then shall ye be blessed in the kingdom of
my Father.

And again, ye shall not have pain while ye shall dwell in the
flesh, neither sorrow, save it be for the sins of the world; and
all this will I do because of the thing which ye have desired
that ye might bring the souls of men unto me, while the
world shall stand. And for this cause ye shall have fullness
of joy; and ye shall sit down in the kingdom of my Father;
yea, your joy shall be full, even as the Father has given me
fullness of joy; and ye shall be even as I am, and I am even as
the Father; and the Father and I are one. And the Holy
Ghost bears record of the Father and me; and the because of
me."

After Jesus spoke these words, He touched each
disciple with His finger, except the three who were to tarry.
Then He departed. The Lord revealed that a change must take
place on the three or they will taste of death. Now this change
was not equal to that which shall take place at the last day;
but there was a change, as much that Satan could have no
power over them, that he could not tempt them. Also, they
were sanctified in the flesh, that they were holy, and that the
powers of the earth could not hold them. Finally, they would
not suffer pain or sorrow, except it was for the sins of the
world. They would remain in this state until the *Judgment
Day* of Christ. At that time, they would receive a greater
change, and be received into the kingdom of the Father.

During their lifetime, the Twelve Disciples were cast
into prison by them who did not belong to the church, but the
prisons could not hold them, for the prisons were torn in two.
As well, the Disciples were buried in the earth; but they smote
the earth with the word of God, so that by His power they were
delivered out of the depths of the earth.

Three times they were cast into a furnace and received
no harm. Twice they were cast into a den of wild beasts; and

behold, they did play with the beasts as a child with a suckling lamb. Eventually, they went forth among all the people and preached the gospel of Christ, and all the people were converted.

The three who would not die are still with us today, somewhere in the world, along with the Apostle John. Interestingly, a Native American in the early nineteenth century, in the State of New York, had a vision of three messengers. These messengers from the Great Spirit said the Native American's life would come to an end when the fourth messenger joined them. (See chapter 16 for more about this American Indian.)

The three Disciples will be among the gentiles and the Jews, but will not be recognized. The day will come when the Lord, in His own wisdom, will allow them to minister to all the tribes of Israel (as well as other people). They will bring many souls to Jesus through the convincing power of God which is in them and so that their desire may be fulfilled. They are as the angels of God, and if they pray to the Father in the name of Jesus, they can show themselves to whomever they choose.

Within a couple of years of Jesus' appearance in the land of America (see the chapter regarding Native American Legends), all of the people were converted to the Lord, both Nephite and Lamanite. There were no contentions, wars or disputations among them. As a matter of fact, the distinction by family name came to an end. Also, there were no rich or poor, bond or free, but they were all made free, and partakers of the heavenly gift.

As time went on, the people rebuilt the cities that had been destroyed. As well, the people became light and delightsome. They no longer performed the ordinances and rituals of the Law of Moses; but they did walk after the commandments that they had received from their Lord and their God, continuing in fasting and prayer, and meeting together to pray and to hear the word of the Lord. The Translated Ancient Nephite Records state that there were never a happier people! What a wonderful condition these people lived in! Yet it is available to us today, if we are obedient to the commandments of God in all things!

Chapter Fourteen

Apostasy, Destruction and Restoration

Two hundred years passed from the sign of Christ's birth and the ancient American people greatly multiplied. They were now spread upon all the face of the land, North, Central and South America. In the year AD 201 there were some who were lifted up in pride, such as wearing expensive apparel, fine jewelry, and other costly, worldly things. So ended the time when they had all things in common. Satan finally made inroads, getting in among them; and the love of God was waxing cold. The people began to be divided into classes. As well, they began to build up churches to get gain. By doing so, they began to deny the true church of Christ. As it turned out, for about 166 years they enjoyed peace, prosperity and the richest blessings of God.

Those churches, which were started by men, denied the true points of Christ's doctrine. To make matters worse, they took in the wicked without repentance and then administered sacred things to those whom it had been forbidden because of unworthiness. Some went so far as to deny even the existence of Christ. These also persecuted the members of the true church of Jesus Christ, who were humble and meek (and who still enjoyed miracles from God).

The Three Disciples who had not died, possibly 210 years old (more or less), were taken by the wicked and were cast into prison; but by the power of the word of God, which was in them, the prisons were torn in two, and they went forth doing mighty miracles among the people. However, the people became so hardened they sought to kill the disciples. The wicked cast the disciples into furnaces of fire, but they were not harmed. They were put in dens of wild beasts and they played with the wild beasts as a child with a lamb.

In the year AD 231 the majority of the people became very wicked, and a division took place. The people once again took their ancestral names. The "new" Lamanites allowed their belief in Christ to dwindle and they openly rebelled against God. The remaining people were the Nephites and were considered the people of God because of their belief in Christ. The three disciples who were not to die, began to feel great sorrow because Satan was greatly influencing the people. They no longer remained among the people who were supposed to be the people of God. (I would like to point out that from time to time the Three Disciples of Christ still appear to Godly men and women throughout the world.)

Wars broke out again between the Nephites and Lamanites. The Lamanites now became a separate and distinct nation of people. They took up the traditions and customs of their forefathers, who in the beginning were rebellious and denied the coming of Christ and the power of God. They became an idle people, full of mischief and subtlety, and hunted for game in the wilderness. Because of their disbelief, they became a dark-skinned people. Any Nephites that mixed or intermarried with the Lamanites became like them.

A man by the name of Mormon, who was born about the year AD 310, was a prophet of God and a disciple of Christ. He became commander-in-chief of the Nephite army or the people of God. He also received the entire history of the Nephite people from a man named Ammaron. (As previously mentioned, that history was written on gold plates in a language called *Reformed Egyptian Characters*. These plates were passed from one generation to the next until Mormon obtained access to them by the will of the Lord. The Prophet abridged these voluminous ancient records onto a new set of plates.)

The young prophet, Mormon, endeavored to preach Christ and righteousness, but the people refused to listen because of the hardness of their hearts. Wickedness prevailed among the Nephites; the gifts and miracles of God disappeared. Even the gift of the Holy Ghost was gone. Sorcery, witchcraft, magic, and the power of evil were upon the whole land: pestilence, famine, and one eternal round of wars replaced the peace and tranquility. Because of these conditions, God would allow the Lamanites to war against them in order to wake them up to their deteriorated situation. By this time, the Lamanites lost all knowledge of the true, living God.

The Lamanites drove the Nephites northward, to a land of many waters, rivers, and fountains. When three hundred and eighty-four years had passed (AD 384), the Nephites gathered all their people together in one place for a final battle. However, the spirit of the Lord was no longer with them and they were left to their own destruction.

Mormon now about seventy-four years old, took the records and hid them all in a hill, with the exception of his abridgment, which he gave to his son, Moroni. At this point in time, the Lamanites far outnumbered the Nephites and a tremendous, grievous battle ensued. Thousands and tens of thousands of them were killed until only twenty-four were left. Finally only one survivor remained, Moroni.

And so was the end of a great civilization in America. The only inhabitants remaining were the Lamanites. They separated into various tribes and clans according to family affiliations. Also, they destroyed the central government of the land. To compensate for that, every tribe appointed a chief or a leader.

As a historical note, through the course of centuries the Lamanites developed distinct tribal languages and dialects, dress, type of habitation, methods of producing or gathering food, and customs and culture. They also had a lot of tribal warfare from time to time. When Columbus arrived in the New World, he thought he had reached the East Indies. For this reason, he called the natives of the New World "Indians."

Moroni finished the record and placed it in a cement-type stone box. He then buried the box in the earth around AD 421. The record remained hid for about fourteen centuries. Around AD 1823, this same man, Moroni, but now a messenger of God, appeared to Joseph Smith, Jr. Moroni not only showed Smith the record, but also instructed him concerning the translation and presentation of the record. Smith did not get possession of the record until AD 1827. He completed the translation by **the gift and the power of God**. The result was *the Translated Ancient Nephite Record*, or what we commonly call the *Book of Mormon*. The name was derived from the last page of the abridged record, which is as follows:

BOOK OF MORMON

AN ACCOUNT WRITTEN BY
THE HAND OF MORMON UPON PLATES
TAKEN FROM THE PLATES OF NEPHI

Wherefore, it is an abridgment of the record of the people of Nephi, and also of the Lamanites.

Written to the Lamanites, who are a remnant of the house of Israel; and also to Jew and Gentile-Written by way of commandment, and also by the spirit of prophecy and of revelation.

Written and sealed up, and hid up unto the Lord, that they might not be destroyed. To come forth by the gift and power of God unto the interpretation thereof.

Sealed by the hand of Moroni, and hid up unto the Lord, to come forth in due time by the way of Gentile, the interpretation thereof by the gift of God.

An abridgment taken from the Book of Ether also, which is a record of the people of Jared, who were scattered at the time the Lord confounded the language of the people, when they were building a tower to get to heaven.

Which is to show unto the remnant of the House of Israel what great things the Lord hath done for their fathers; and that they may know the covenants of the Lord, that they are not cast off forever.

And also to the convincing of the Jew and Gentile that Jesus is the Christ, the Eternal God, manifesting himself unto all nations.

And now, if there are faults they are the mistakes of men. Wherefore, condemn not the things of God that ye may be found spotless at the judgment seat of Christ.

Moroni

Translated by Joseph Smith, Jr.

Published by

THE CHURCH OF JESUS CHRIST

Monongahela, Pennsylvania 15063

As I stated before, and as can be seen by the above, the Book of Mormon contains the history of the migration of two Israelite families to America, their civilization, history, and wars, and the origin of the American Indians, as well as their destiny. I would like to quote some very important words recorded by Mormon before his death in the great, final battle:

> My soul is rent with anguish because of the slain of my people. 0 ye fair ones, how could ye have departed from the ways of the Lord! 0 ye fair ones [Nephites], how could ye have rejected that Jesus, who stood with open arms to receive you? Behold, if ye had not done this, ye would not have fallen. But behold, ye are fallen, and I mourn your loss. 0 ye fair sons and daughters, ye fathers and mothers, ye husbands and wives, ye fair ones, how is it that ye could have fallen! But ye are gone, and my sorrows cannot bring your return.

> And the day soon comes that your mortal being must put on immortality, and these bodies which are now smoldering in corruption must soon become incorruptible bodies; and then ye must stand before the judgment seat of Christ to be judged according to your works; and if it so be that ye are righteous, then are ye blessed with your fathers who had gone before you. O that ye had repented before this great destruction had come upon you! But behold, ye are gone, and the Father of Heaven knows your state; and He does with you according to His mercy and justice.

Mormon now speaks to the Lamanites (Native Americans) of our day and time, when his record would come forth and reveal the history of the Native Americans and begin the process of **restoration,** saying,

> I speak to you, the remnant of the house of Israel [Lamanites; Native Americans]. Know ye not that you are of the house of Israel. Know ye that you must come unto repentance, or ye cannot be saved. Know ye that ye must lay down your weapons of war, and delight no more in the shedding of blood, and take them not again, except that God shall command you.

> Know ye that ye must come to the knowledge of your fathers, and repent of all your sins and iniquities, and believe in Jesus Christ, that He is the Son of God, and that He was put on the cross, died, and by the power of the Father, He has

risen again, whereby He has gained the victory over the grave; and also in Him is the sting of death swallowed up. And He brings to pass the resurrection of the dead, whereby man must be raised to stand before his judgment seat. And He has brought to pass the redemption of the world, he that is found guiltless before Him at the Judgment Day will be given to dwell in the presence of God in His kingdom, to sing ceaseless praises with the choirs above, unto the Father, and unto the Son, and unto the Holy Ghost, which are one God, and in a state of happiness which has no end.

Now I would add my concurrence with those words and encourage everyone to repent and be baptized in the name of Jesus Christ, and lay hold upon the gospel of Christ, which shall be set before you, not only in this record (Translated Ancient Nephite Record), but also in the Bible. Both of these will come to you by the gentiles (European-Americans). If you believe this, you will know concerning your fathers, and also the marvelous works which were wrought by the power of God among them. Mormon also states:

And you will also know that you are a remnant of the seed of Jacob [posterity, Israelites]; therefore you are numbered among the people of the first covenant; and if it so be that you believe in Christ, and are baptized, first with water, then with fire and with the Holy Ghost, following the example of our Savior, according to that which He had commanded us it shall be well with you in the day of the judgment. Amen.

What beautiful words this prophet uttered before his death. If only Americans would adhere to these words, they could avoid the impending destruction of this nation, because of the abounding violence, corruption, and sin. This applies not only to our country, but to all the inhabitants of the world. The only solution for the ills of the world is Jesus Christ.

Now here are the words of the last surviving prophet, Moroni, son of Mormon:

Behold, I finish the record of my father, I have but a few things to write, which things I have been commanded by my father. After the great and tremendous battle, the Nephites who had escaped into the country southward were hunted by the Lamanites, until they were all destroyed. Now whether they will slay me, I know not.

However, I will write and hide up the records in the earth; and where I go it matters not. I have no friends or kinsfolk, and how long the Lord will suffer that I may live I know not. The Lamanites have hunted my people from city to city and from place to place, even until they are no more; and great has been their fall, and destruction of my people, a white and fair people. It was the judgment of the Lord upon them. There are none that know the true, living God, except the three disciples of Jesus who are still living. My father and I have seen them and they have ministered unto us.

Keep in mind that those Three Disciples would be approximately three hundred and eighty years old (more or less). And remember, they are still somewhere upon the earth, appearing to whomever God will have them appear.

Moroni continued his exhortation and prediction concerning the coming forth of the record:

Who so receives this record [Translated Ancient American Record] shall not condemn it because of the imperfections which are in it. The same shall know of greater things than these. Were it possible, I would make all things known unto you. I am the same who hides up this record unto the Lord; the plates thereof are of no worth, because of the commandment of the Lord. For He truly says that no one shall have them to get gain; but the record is of great worth; and who so shall bring it to light, him will the Lord bless [the translator, Joseph Smith, Jr.]. And blessed be he who shall bring this thing to light; for it shall be brought out of darkness unto light, according to the word of God; yea, it shall be brought *out of the earth.*

I want to point out that the prophecy of Psalms 85:11 was fulfilled with the coming forth of the *Book of Mormon,* since the record was buried in the earth.

Now Moroni continued saying,

And it shall shine forth out of darkness, and come unto the knowledge of the people [gentiles, Jews, American Indians]. It shall be done by the power of God. And if there be faults, they be the faults of a man. But behold, we know no fault; nevertheless, God knows all things; therefore, he that condemns, let him be aware lest he shall be in danger of hell fire.

And no one need say they shall not come, for they surely shall, for the Lord hath spoken it; for out of the earth shall they come, by the hand of the Lord, and none can stay it. And it shall come in a day when it shall be said that miracles, gifts, and visions are done away with. It shall come in a day of secret combinations [organized crime and cartels] and the works of darkness [corruption, bribery, blackmail]. Yea, it shall come in a day when the power of God shall be denied, and churches become defiled and be lifted up in the pride of their hearts; yea, even in a day when leaders of churches and teachers shall rise in the pride of their hearts, even to the envying of them who belong to their churches.

As well as warning us of the religious and social conditions of the day, the prophet also depicts the natural environment. Listen to this prophecy.

Yea, it shall come in a day when there shall be heard of fires, tempest, and vapors of smoke in foreign lands. Wars, rumors of wars, and earthquakes in diverse places. Yea, it shall come in a day when there shall be great pollution upon the face of the earth. Yea, it shall come in a day when there shall be murders, thefts, lying, deceiving, whoredom, and all manner of abominations; and many will say, do this, or do that, and it matters not, for the Lord will uphold such at the last day. But woe unto such for they are in the gall of bitterness and in the bonds of iniquity. Yea, it shall come in a day when churches shall say, 'come unto me, and for your money you shall be forgiven of your sins.'

And I know that you walk in the pride of your hearts, wearing very fine apparel, envying, strife, malice, persecutions and all manner of iniquities. For behold, you do love money, and your substance, and your fine apparel, the adorning of your churches more than you love the poor and the needy, the sick and the afflicted. Behold, the judgment of God hangs over you, and to you who deny the God of the heavens and the earth and the Son of God, when you see the judgments of God come upon you and brought before the judgment seat. Then will you say that there is no God?

Could anything be plainer than this? The pollution on the earth is obvious. There is pollution of air, water, and land.

There is pollution of the mind because of evil and sinful thoughts. There is pollution of the eye through obscenity, pornography, and lust. There is pollution of mouth due to lying, dirty speech, and profanity. There is pollution of hands via murder and theft. And there is pollution of heart because of carnal, devilish, sensual, and high-minded intentions and desires. Moroni has some more to say.

> And to you who deny the revelations of God and say they are done away with. Or the gifts, prophecies, healing, visions, angels, speaking tongues and the interpretation of tongues are done away with, do not know the Gospel of Christ, or have not read the Scriptures; if so, do not understand them. For we read in the Bible that God is the same yesterday, today, and forever. And in Him there is no variableness, neither shadow of changing. If the gifts and miracles cease, then He would cease to be God. However, God never changes, only man changes. If the gifts are done away with, it is because of unbelief and lack of faith.

As he completed the record (around AD 421) Moroni said, "And now I bid unto all farewell. I soon go to rest in the Paradise of God, until my spirit and body shall again reunite, and I am brought forth triumphant through the air, to meet you before the pleasing bar of the great Jehovah, the Eternal Judge of both quick and dead. Amen."

Since my purpose in this chapter is to show the falling away or apostasy of the true Church of Jesus Christ (and I believe I have done so by showing you the collapse of the Nephite nation and their religious turmoil), I want to share with you an epistle or religious letter, written by Mormon, the commander of the Nephite armies and the person who abridged the records of the Nephite people. In this epistle, Mormon explains to his son, Moroni, the doctrine of **blessing**, not baptizing, children (compare with Matthew 19:13-15). Baptizing of children is **not** the doctrine of Christ and is a perversion of the Gospel.

> Now, my son, I have learned that there is disputation among you concerning the baptism of your little children. I desire that this gross error should be removed from among you. I inquired of the Lord concerning this matter. And the word of the Lord came to me by the power of the Holy Ghost, saying, 'Listen to the words of Christ, your Redeemer, your Lord and your God. Behold, I came into the world not to call the

righteous but sinners to repentance; the whole need no physician, but they that are sick; wherefore, little children are whole, for they are not capable of committing sin; wherefore the curse of Adam is taken from them in me, that it has no power over them; and the law of circumcision is done away in me. I know that it is solemn mockery before God, that ye should baptize little children.

Behold, I say unto you that ye teach repentance and baptism unto those who are accountable and capable of committing sin; teach parents that they must repent and humble themselves as their little children and they shall be saved with their children. Little children are alive in Christ, even from the foundation of the world. Behold, I say unto you, he that supposes that little children need baptism is in the gall of bitterness and in the bonds of iniquity, for he has neither faith, hope, nor charity; wherefore he will be cut off while in the thought, he must go down to hell. Woe unto them that shall pervert the ways of the Lord. I speak with boldness, having authority from God; and I fear not what man can do; for perfect love casts out all fear.

I would also like to expand on the concept of *a restoration*. This concept encompasses two general aspects: spiritual and natural. The spiritual restoration includes the restoring of the power and authority of God to the earth, the establishing of the true points of Christ's gospel, and the organizing of the body of Christ, or The Church of Jesus Christ, built upon His restored gospel and authority. The impetus of the spiritual restoration was the coming forth of the Book of Mormon (Translated Ancient Nephite Record) in 1827-1830. This record, when combined with the Bible, confounded the false teachings and doctrines of men.

The second restoration aspect is the natural restoration. This aspect includes a restoration of Native Americans' knowledge of their forefathers, their history and their future. It also envelops the return of the Native Americans' lands of inheritance (their homelands in the Americas) and the building of the *New Jerusalem* described in the prior chapter. Finally, the natural restoration includes the restoration of all of the tribes of Israel to a true knowledge of God and their lands of inheritance. So we can see, as terrible and sad as the destruction of the great Ancient Indian civilizations and the corruption and apostasy of the Church of Jesus Christ were, the promise of the restoration of The

Church of Jesus Christ and the whole House of Israel, beginning with the Lamanites (seed of Joseph; American Indians), as well as the building of a *New Society* (a term used in some ancient Indian prophecies), is wondrous and marvelous.

The Prophet Isaiah actually uses those words in describing these events, when the Lord spoke to him saying, "Therefore, behold, I will proceed to do a marvelous work among this people, even a marvelous work and a wonder: for the wisdom of their wise men shall perish, and the understanding of their prudent men shall be hid." For more information regarding the Restoration, I encourage the reader to read other booklets published by The Church of Jesus Christ, Monongahela, Pennsylvania.

I would also like to point out that between the time of the destruction of the Nephite people and the restoration of the Lamanites to a true knowledge of their ancestors and the Book of Mormon, they have undergone and will undergo a terrible punishment through oppression by the Europeans who came to America. The Lamanites were driven about as chaff before the wind, or, as a vessel is tossed about upon the waves, without sail, anchor, or helm to steer her. They were also placed on reserves/reservations (in the US and Canada) and are still killed in some Central American countries.

However, the time is approaching, and is nigh at the door, when God will raise up a leader among them, a righteous and Godly person to fulfill the prophecies concerning their restoration to the land of their inheritance. And they shall become a white and delightsome people of the Lord. And they shall believe in the true, living God and in His beloved Son, the Lord Jesus Christ – the God of Abraham, Isaac, and Jacob, the God who created the heavens and the earth, and all the things that are in it. And now let's take a look at that leader who God will raise-up.

Chapter Fifteen

American Indian Moses

In previous chapters I referred to the records that were brought to America by the Israelite colony, and they were called the *Jerusalem Brass Plates*. This record contained the genealogy of the prophet Lehi and the Hebrew Scriptures. But just as important, there was also a prediction, not found in the Bible, of the coming forth of an *American Indian Moses*. This is the subject that I have been leading up to. So, let us delve into it now.

Between 588 and 570 BC the prophet Lehi related to his son Joseph the prophecy, saying, "I am a descendant of Joseph who was sold by his brethren and carried into Egypt. And great were the covenants of the Lord which He made to Joseph." We will now examine the prophecy of Joseph taken from the *Jerusalem Brass Plates* as the prophet Lehi gave it to his son.

> Joseph [of Egypt] truly saw our day. And he obtained a promise from the Lord, that out of the fruit of his loins [posterity] the Lord God would raise up a righteous branch unto the house of Israel [the purpose of the migration to America] – not the Messiah, but a branch which was to be broken off, nevertheless, to be remembered in the covenants of the Lord. And the Messiah should be made manifest unto them in the latter days [near future] in the spirit of power, unto the bringing of them out of darkness unto light-yea, out of hidden darkness and out of captivity unto freedom. A *SEER* shall the Lord my God raise up, who shall be a *CHOICE SEER* out of the fruit of my loins [from Joseph of Egypt to Lehi and out of his posterity the American Lamanites].

> And he shall be esteemed highly among the fruit of thy loins [Native Americans]. And unto him will I give commandment that he shall do a work for the fruit of his loins, his brethren, which shall be of great worth unto them, even to the bringing of them to the knowledge of the covenants which I have made with thy fathers. And I will give unto him a commandment that he shall do none other work, except the work which I shall command him. And I will make him great in mine eyes; for he shall do my work. And he shall be great like unto Moses, whom I have said I would raise up unto you, to

deliver my people, 0 House of Israel. And a Moses will I raise up, to deliver thy people out of the land of Egypt.

But a *SEER* will I raise up out of the fruit of thy loins [Native Americans] and unto him will I give power to bring forth my word unto the seed of thy loins-and not to the bringing forth my word only, saith the Lord, but to the convincing them of my word, which shall have already gone forth among them. Wherefore, the fruit of thy loins shall write [Ancient Nephite Records] and the fruit of the loins of Judah shall write [Jews, Bible] and that which shall be written by the fruit of thy loins, and also that which shall be written by the fruit of the loins of Judah, shall grow together, unto the confounding of false doctrines and laying down of contentions, and establishing peace among the fruit of thy loins [Native Americans], and bringing them to the knowledge of their fathers in the latter days, and also to the knowledge of my covenants, saith the Lord. And out of weakness he shall be made strong, in that day when my work shall commence among all my people, unto the restoring thee, 0 House of Israel, saith the Lord.

And thus prophesied Joseph saying, "Behold, that *SEER* will the Lord bless; and they that seek to destroy him shall be confounded; for this promise, which I have obtained of the Lord, of the fruit of my loins, shall be fulfilled. Behold, I am sure of the fulfilling of this promise. And his name shall be called after me; and it shall be after the name of his father. And he shall be like unto me; for the thing, which the Lord shall bring forth by His hand, by the power of the Lord shall bring my people unto salvation." Yea, thus prophesied Joseph [of Egypt], "I am sure of this thing, even as I am sure of the promise of Moses; for the Lord hath said unto me, I will preserve thy seed forever."

And the Lord had said, "I will raise up a Moses; and I will give power unto him in a rod; and I will give judgment unto him in writing. Yet I will not loose his tongue, that he shall speak much, for I will not make him mighty in speaking. But I will write unto him my law, by the finger of mine own hand; and I will make a spokesman for him." [You that are acquainted with the story of Moses know how the Lord provided a spokesman for him, Aaron his brother.] And the Lord said, "I will raise up [a Moses] unto the fruit of thy loins [American Indian]. And I will make for him a spokesman [a person who will speak for the *SEER*... And behold, I will give unto him that he shall write the writing of the fruit of thy loins, unto

111

the fruit of thy loins; and the spokesman of thy loins shall declare it. And the words which he shall write shall be the words which are expedient in my wisdom should go forth unto the fruit of thy loins. And it shall be as if the fruit of thy loins had cried unto them from the dust; for I know their faith.

And they shall cry from the dust; yea, even repentance unto their brethren, even after many generations have gone by them. And it shall come to pass that their cry shall go, even according to the simpleness of their words. Because of their faith, their words shall proceed forth out of my mouth unto their brethren who are the fruit of thy loins; and the weakness of their words will I make strong in their faith, unto the remembering of my covenant which I made unto thy fathers. And now, my son, after this manner did my father of old prophesy. Wherefore, because of this covenant thou art blessed; for thy seed shall not be destroyed, for they shall hearken unto the words of the book.

And there shall rise up one mighty among them, who shall do much good, both in word and in deed, being an instrument in the hands of God, with exceeding faith, to work mighty wonders, and do that thing which is great in the sight of God, into the bringing to pass much restoration unto the house of Israel, and unto the seed of thy brethren."

I will now provide an explanation of the prediction concerning the *CHOICE SEER* or as I call him, the **American Indian Moses.**

The prophet Lehi told his son Joseph about their forefather, Joseph. This Joseph, the son of Jacob, was the one sold by his brothers and eventually became second in command in all of Egypt. Lehi explained to his son that they were descendants of that Joseph and that God had made great promises to him. Joseph was not only a great administrator (as Pharaoh discovered) but also a prophet of God. He saw the future including Lehi and Lehi's descendants (American Indians). Joseph obtained a specific promise from the Lord, that out of his posterity, God would raise up a righteous branch of the house of Israel. This branch was not the Israelites from whom the Messiah would be born, but a branch that was to be broken off or separated from the land of Canaan via a migration to America. Although separated, these people would be remembered in the covenants of the Lord.

One of the other promises is that the Messiah (Christ) would be manifested to them in the latter days in the spirit of power in bringing them out of darkness into light and out of captivity to freedom. As we saw in the prior chapters, the condition of the Lamanites or Native Americans is bad. For them to become a blessed and favored people, God will need to do a great work among them. But this work cannot come from the gentiles (European-Americans) only. Instead, Joseph (of Egypt) saw that a Native American would do the Lord's work. Joseph testified that God would raise a SEER up. This seer would be a **choice** seer for several reasons. But before I explain what those reasons are, I should explain what a seer is.

The Translated Ancient Nephite Record states that a seer is like a prophet, except with a greater gift of being able to not only see the future, but to see the past. He can also translate ancient records by the gift and power of God through the use of *interpreters*. These fascinating instruments were described in the Book of Mormon as "two stones which were fastened into the two rims of a bow" (almost as a pair of glasses).

I would like to point out that Joseph Smith, Jr. was a seer because he had these unique tools to translate the Book of Mormon, but he was **not** the Choice Seer prophesied by Joseph of Egypt. Some people make this mistake. The Choice Seer foretold by Joseph was to come out of his posterity, that is, he would be a Native American. Additionally, the Choice Seer would be esteemed (venerated, distinguished, respected) among the Native Americans, his own people. This did not occur with Joseph Smith, Jr. Records indicate that Joseph Smith, Jr. may never have even preached to any Native Americans.

In essence the Choice Seer will be a benefactor for his people, as well as obedient to the laws of Christ; a man who will embrace the true gospel of Jesus Christ and be chosen by the Lord. God will give him power and authority to do the work of the Lord, but only the work the Lord assigns him, as the prophecy says, "And to him will I give commandments that he shall do work for his brethren, which shall be of great worth unto them, even to the bringing of them to the knowledge of the covenants which I have made with thy fathers."

Included in this work are the Choice Seer's efforts to unite the Native Americans as one people under the Gospel of Jesus Christ. Although they may maintain for a period of time their identity as tribes and their tribal culture, eventually they will unite as a nation of people and abandon the tradition and customs of their forefathers that were adopted when they lost the knowledge of the true, living God.

The Lord will also make this Choice Seer great in the Lord's eyes, not necessarily in the eyes of men. Why? Because he will only do the work commissioned him by God and not by man. Often, prophets and seers in ancient times were greatly persecuted when they were obedient to the will of God. Even Jesus Christ noted that many prophets were killed and they are not without honor, except in their own community. So it is possible that many gentiles (non-Indians) will take offense at the words and work of the Choice Seer because he will be strictly working for the Lord.

Here is part of the prophecy I want you to take special notice of: "And he shall be great like unto *MOSES,* whom I have said I would raise up unto you to deliver my people, 0 House of Israel. And *MOSES* will I raise up, to deliver the Israelites out of the land of Egypt, from slavery and bondage." This prediction states that the Choice Seer or **American Indian Moses** will be great like the Jewish Moses, whom the Lord said He would use to deliver the Israelites from their Egyptian bondage (which was fulfilled).

The prophecy of Joseph notes that God will give power to the Choice Seer to bring God's word to the Native American, and to the convincing them of the word. Now, I want to point out that the prophecy states that the word will have already gone forth among the Native Americans. What this means is that prior to the arrival of the Choice Seer, the gentiles (non-Israelites) will have the Translated Ancient Nephite Record and will share it with the Native Americans. The Choice Seer will convince the Native Americans of the truth of these scriptures. Then he will bring forth more of God's word and provide greater details and clarity to the word of God already in our possession. That is why I and the church that I am affiliated with endeavor to share the message of the Book of Mormon, the past and future of Native Americans, and the coming of the Choice Seer, with Native Americans everywhere.

Lehi also related the prophecy regarding the relationship between the Book of Mormon and the Bible. The prophecy states that the posterity of Joseph (of Egypt) through the posterity of the Prophet Lehi will write the Nephite Record and the Jews in Jerusalem will write the Bible. These two records or books will grow together, to the confounding of false doctrines, and eliminating contentions and establishing peace among the gentiles and the Native Americans. It will also inform them of their forefathers and the covenants of the Lord to them.

The Prophet Lehi continued by noting that the American Indian Moses will be made strong by the Lord, in the day when the Lord's work will commence among His people, to the restoring of the House of Israel. Joseph said "Behold, that seer will the Lord bless, and they that seek to destroy him shall be confounded; for this promise I have obtained from the Lord. Behold, I am sure of the fulfilling of this promise. These things that shall come forth by the power of the Lord to bring salvation to his people."

Separately, Joseph was promised by God that the Lord, would "raise up Moses and give him power in a rod and I will give him judgment in writing. Yet I will not loose his tongue to speak much or make him mighty in speaking, but I will write unto him my law, by the finger of my own hand, I will make a spokesman for him [Aaron, his brother]."

Likewise, the Lord said, he would raise up among the Native Americans a spokesman for the Choice Seer. The Seer will write what the Lord commands him to write and the spokesman will declare it. And the words he will write will be expedient in God's wisdom, and will go forth to the Native Americans. Because of the faith of the Ancient Native Americans (Nephites and Lamanites), their words will go forth among the modern Native American nations and the faithful among them will be made strong in remembering the covenants God made with their forefathers.

Lehi then added a prophecy, not given to Joseph, nor found in the *Jerusalem Brass Plates*. He stated that a Native American will come who will do much good, both in word and in deed, being an instrument in the hands of God. He will have exceeding faith, to work mighty wonders, and do that thing which is great in the sight of God, in bringing to pass much restoration to the house of Israel, and to the Native Americans.

I began this book with the origin of the Jews and especially the man Moses, how God selected this man to become the Deliverer of the Israelites in the land of Egypt, as well as a few predictions of their restoration in the latter days. God is working today to bring about the covenants that He had made to Abraham, Isaac, and Jacob (Israel). I have also written the prediction of Joseph (of Egypt) concerning the coming forth of a *CHOICE SEER, DELIVERER,* and, as I term it, *AMERICAN INDIAN MOSES* in the near future.

Speaking of a *DELIVERER,* the Apostle Paul made a prediction in the eleventh chapter of Paul's letter to the Romans; verse twenty-six, which I am convinced, refers to the American Indian Moses. Let me quote it: "And so all Israel shall be saved: as it is written, there shall come out of Zion [America] the *DELIVERER,* and shall turn away ungodliness from Jacob." Paul cannot be referring to Jesus Christ, as he had already come, but Paul is referring to another man. Also, in the New Testament, the term deliverer was not applied to Jesus as it was to Moses.

Another scripture I believe refers to the *CHOICE SEER* which is found in the Book of Genesis, chapter forty-nine, verse twenty-four: "From thence is the shepherd, the stone of Israel." As we know, Jacob bestowed the blessing of the Messiah on the tribe of Judah. This prophecy refers to someone from the tribe of Joseph. Verse twenty-two of the same chapter even tells us where. It reads, "Joseph [of Egypt] is a fruitful bough, even a fruitful bough by a well; whose branches [posterity] run over the wall [oceanic migration to America]."

The last surviving Nephite wrote the following words:

And when ye shall receive these things, I would exhort you that ye would ask God, the Eternal Father, in the name of Christ, if these things are not true; and if ye shall ask with a sincere heart, with real intent, having faith in Christ, he will manifest the truth of it unto you, by the power of the Holy Ghost. And by the power of the Holy Ghost ye may know the truth of all things.

And whatsoever thing is good is just and true; wherefore, nothing that is good denies the Christ, but acknowledges that he is. And ye may know that he is, by the power of the Holy Ghost; wherefore I would exhort you that ye deny not the power of God; for he works by power, according to the faith of the children of men, the same today and tomorrow, and forever.

The **American Indian Moses** is going to be an extraordinary man in the hands of God. It is essential that someone like Moses arise from among the Native Americans, in order to unite them as a nation and a people, to demonstrate to them that God has not forgotten them. I am deeply and personally convinced with profound faith in the fulfillment of this prophecy in the near future. The events that are transpiring in the world concerning the house of Israel are unquestionably fulfilling the scriptures. The events that are transpiring in Americas concerning the Native American are also fulfilling scriptures and prophecies. I urge you to keep an eye on the events transpiring among the Indians in the present and the future.

Here is an excerpt from a prophecy given by Joseph Smith, Jr. back in 1832: "And it shall come to pass also that the remnants [Indians] who are left on the land will marshal themselves, and shall become exceedingly angry, and shall vex the gentiles [Americans] with a sore vexation." This vexation is due to the injustices, oppression, and discriminations foisted against Native Americans since the sixteenth century.

I say to the Native American, seek the Great Spirit, the God of the heavens and the earth and His beloved Son, the Lord and Savior Jesus Christ, and ask if these things are not true. And if you ask with a sincere heart, with real intent, having faith in Christ, He will manifest the truth of it unto you, by the power of the Holy Ghost. And by the power of the Holy Ghost you may know the truth of all things. Deny not the power of the Great Spirit, for He works by power, according to the faith of the children of men, the same today, tomorrow and forever. And do not deny the gifts of God, for they are many.

Over the years, alcohol and drug abuse have greatly afflicted Native Americans. Much of it can be attributed to the terrible economic state that the Native American has been forced into. At the time Columbus came to America, the Native Americans did not have a concept of land ownership; no one person owned any land. Everyone enjoyed the fruits and bounties of the land. The European culture was far different. This difference led to the taking of Native American territories. Initially it was taken little by little. But as the appetite for land of the colonists increased, so did the taking of it. When simple barter did not produce quick enough results, then armed force was employed. Eventually, the Native Americans in the United States and Canada were placed on *reserves/reservations*. All of their former culture and customs ignored, ridiculed and despised by the European-Americans.

You have heard the term *Forgotten Americans*. This term is aptly applied when it is related to our government's management of the Native American from the eighteenth century until today. But they are not forgotten to the Great Spirit; he has not forgotten them despite their sufferings down through the years. The time is drawing near when God will take a direct hand in the matter. However, the Native American must come to the Great Spirit in righteousness and the righteous among the European-Americans must share with them the true, pure gospel of Christ, both by word and by action.

When the first European explorers set foot on the Western Hemisphere, Christian missionaries accompanied them. These missionaries attempted to convert the Indians. At the same time, the explorers, particularly those of Spain (Conquistadors), savagely treated the Native Americans as slaves. Over the years there were lies, atrocities, and broken treaties. Today, for us to approach the Native American with the great story of the Translated Ancient Nephite Record, we must walk-the-talk, that is, demonstrate our beliefs as living examples of the doctrine of Christ. Then they will be willing to hear the message about their ancestors and about their glorious future.

And what is that example that we (gentiles) should set? How about the fruit of the spirit! What is the fruit of the spirit? Let the Apostle Paul answer this question. "The fruit of the spirit is love, joy, peace, long-suffering, gentleness, goodness, faith, meekness, temperance: against such there is no law." Just so that we are clear, I want to tell you what the other side of the coin is: the works of the flesh. These are: "adultery, fornication, uncleanness, lasciviousness, idolatry, witchcraft, hatred, variance, emulation, wrath, strife, sedition, heresy, envying, murder, drunkenness, reveling, and such: of which I tell you before, as I have also told you in time past, that they which do such things shall not inherit the kingdom of God."

As I previously stated, the Lord God designated this land after the receding of the floodwaters to be the home of a righteous and holy people. And when sin prevails and becomes the norm, the Lord will strike this land with great and awful judgment. And after the judgment of God has been fulfilled, then comes the reign of peace in righteousness that we previously discussed (often called the **Peaceful Reign**, or **Zion** in America or the **Stone Kingdom**5). This reign will be for the Western Hemisphere for a long period of time. And not only will this land be returned to the Native American as their land of inheritance, but it will become a haven for all righteous gentiles and Jews. And, as I pointed out in the prior chapter, it will become the location of the establishment of the **New Jerusalem**, a holy city to God in America.

Abraham Lincoln in his Proclamation of 1863 declared that nations as well as men should confess their sins and transgressions in humble sorrow, yet with assured hope that genuine repentance will lead to mercy and pardon. Nations are blessed whose God is the Lord. And we Americans have been the recipients of the choicest bounties of Heaven. We have grown in numbers, wealth, and power as no other nation has ever grown. Have we forgotten God? The Book of Mormon (Translated Ancient Nephite Record) states that we must worship the God of this land, Jesus Christ, or we will be doomed to destruction. Lincoln, in time of distress, sorrow, and the tremendous burden of the Civil War, unquestionably turned to his God. He confessed the divine sovereignty of the Almighty God.

It is quite interesting that after such presidential policies as the Square Deal, the New Deal, the New Frontier and the Great Society and the political activism of the Christian Coalition and other religious bodies, that the same old social ills and problems, such as prejudice, discrimination, violence, poverty, abortion, illiteracy, teenage pregnancy and pornography have not been solved. Why? The scriptures say, "Because the love of many has waxed cold." It takes the love of God in the hearts of men and women to solve the problems that we are confronted with in the world. Pride, nationality, or race is no excuse. We are one in the sight of God when it comes to salvation, rights, and liberties. I believe it is most appropriate that races should cleave together, and be proud of their race, helping one another. But it cannot become a facade or mask for evil, injustice, laziness, or oppression. We must become spiritually industrious. A new **spiritual culture** must be adopted, one based on the Holy Scriptures and which is rooted in the commandments of God; a culture that has Jesus Christ as its leader and is imbued with the Spirit of God.

We are aware that injustices have been done to minorities and nationalities, including the African American, the Jew, and most inconspicuously, the Native American. Many have emerged from these injustices by helping themselves and others through education and good citizenship. In some instances prejudice, discrimination, and hatred have been replaced with goodwill. But evil is still abundant and the efforts of people are not sufficient. Private and public destruction, vandalism, rioting, civil disobedience, violence, and war do not solve anything; they simply worsen the situation.

Victims of such conditions suffer untold misery and death, without improving anyone's position or status. As the Lord told Moroni, "And if men come unto me I will show unto them their weakness. I give unto men weakness that they may be humble; and my grace is sufficient for all men that humble themselves before me; for if they humble themselves before me, and have faith in me, then will I make weak things become strong unto them." Or as the Apostle Paul wrote, "I can do all things through Christ who strengthens me."

Salvation is for all races of people who are obedient to the laws of Christ. God does not look on the color or appearance, whether an individual is handsome or not. He looks at the hearts of men. When the prophet, Samuel, was to anoint a new king for Israel, he looked at the appearance of several young men, but God spoke to Samuel and said, "Look not on his countenance, or on the height of his stature; because I have refused him: for the Lord sees not as man sees; for man looks on the outward appearance, but the Lord looks on the heart." The Bible says, "He that believes and is baptized [and endures to the end] is saved; he that believes not is damned." The fundamental doctrine of Christ in the Bible is, faith, repentance, adult baptism by immersion, and the laying on of hands for the reception of the Holy Ghost. (Baptism and reception of the Holy Ghost must be performed by one duly authorized from heaven to do such.)

I also want to note that it is apparent that there is a deterioration of godly principles and moral decay in the home and work place in this affluent society of ours. Fathers and mothers should be an example of good citizenship, discipline, and love. Parents should love one another, and their children, in good times and bad.

Civil laws are for the benefit of mankind, but in and of themselves cannot bring order and righteousness, even if many are based on Godly law. There needs to be a truly high standard of integrity and morality from within the person. As Jesus pointed out, it was not what went into a person that defiles them, but what comes out of their heart. Also, he noted that where your treasure is, there will your heart be also and a good man out of the good treasure of the heart brings forth good things: and an evil man out of the evil treasure brings forth evil things.

Of course, laws are only as good as those who are to enforce them. Judges who are supposed to judge the lawbreakers have become corrupt. And the lawyers who are to represent the accused and the law, self-deal and seek personal gain more often than not. Even people who work for law enforcement agencies have become the focus of investigation because of their corruption. And none of this addresses the drug traffickers, organized crime, or other secret and evil groups. I ask, how long shall a nation survive when internal decay persists? In Proverbs we read, "Righteousness exalts a nation: but sin is a reproach to any people." When it comes to sin, God does not respect nations or persons. Here's what the Apostle Peter said, by the spirit of the Lord: "Of a truth I perceive that God does not respect persons: but in every nation he that fears him, and works righteousness, is accepted with Him." Hatred and violence among the people of the world must be replaced with the love for God, country, and fellow man, and obedience to the Prince of Peace, Jesus Christ. Now is the time to seek a spiritual solution to the social ills of our world. As the Prophet Isaiah wrote: "Seek the Lord while he may be found; call upon him while he is near." Jesus warned that the time of darkness would come when no one would have a chance to change his or her ways. We cannot delay!

Chapter Sixteen

Other Evidences

I would like to present to the reader some additional evidence that confirms the material I have presented from the Bible and Book of Mormon. This evidence is in the form of ancient American Indian legends and personal observations and conversations I have had with Native Americans. Generally, legends are not used as evidence, since often they are considered fanciful or fictitious. However, as most scholars will confirm, many legends are born out of truth or actual events. So I would like to present some legends of significance.

In a book titled *Cry of the Ancients* (Herald House, Independence, Missouri, 1974), the authors, Grey Owl and Little Pigeon, presented the following:

> During his travels, Grey Owl made many friends among the various tribes, and they often sat for hours comparing legends and traditions as well as their present-day problems. He noticed that although nature legends often differed, and historical tradition told of different experience, all the tribes shared one common memory – that of a wonderful prophet and teacher, a holy man who walked among the people in ages long gone by. Though he was called by various names and the stories differed from tribe to tribe, all agreed upon this point: the Divine Visitor was pale of skin, had sea-green eyes, and a beard and hair of copper color.

> Always he taught the lessons of love and peace, of man's obligation to his fellowman, and of the love of the Father-of-all for his children. It was he who had instituted all our finer impulses of concern for one another.

> The following was a legend Grey Owl had heard and had never seen written anywhere else:

> It is said that once very long ago before the coming of the white man, long before the time of our grandfather's grandfathers, a stranger came to our people. He appeared suddenly, as they were gathered about the council fire; and at first the people were much afraid, thinking him to be a

spirit. It is said that he was of strange appearance, that his skin was pale as a ghost and there was hair upon his face.

But soon they saw that they had nothing to fear, for he said that he had come from the Great Spirit to teach them to live in love together. Food was brought to him, and as he ate he told many stories of a land far away across the water where people had become very wicked. He said he had many enemies but the worst of these was the Spirit of Evil who led men astray and caused them to hate each other.

It is said he taught many things about medicine and healing and repeated to them many rituals. At last one of the people asked by what name he might be called and he answered that wherever he traveled, men gave him a name according to their language. At this, the people told him, "It is our custom to use the names given to us in our childhood." They would prefer to use the name by which he was known in his own country. And the name he left them was Ye-Sos -- Ye-Sos Gah-lis-tos.

I have previously mentioned about the Native American in New York State who had the dream of the three messengers, later joined by the fourth. This man's name was *Handsome Lake* and he was born near the Genesee River around 1735. He was the half-brother of the famous Native American, *Cornplanter*. Handsome Lake, based on the message of the three personages, taught *Gai-wiio* to the Indians of the Iroquois Confederacy. Often it is referred to as the *Code of Handsome Lake*. The messengers who appeared to Handsome Lake stated that they were ordained by the Creator to appear to men at certain times of need to offer aid and to teach again the laws by which men ought to live. How fascinating that this account mirrors the words in the Translated Ancient Nephite Record regarding the Three Disciples of Christ in Ancient America.

Handsome Lake also had a vision of *Segan'-hedus*, that is, *He Who Resurrects*. The following is the account of their meeting:

The four messengers had conducted the prophet [Handsome Lake] through a series of visions and now they passed a man who paused to ask a question of him. "Did you never hear your grandfathers say that once there was a certain man upon the earth across the great waters who was slain by his

123

own people?" The prophet answered that yes, he had heard this story from his grandparents [meaning their ancient traditions]. "I am he," proclaimed the stranger, "Segan'-hedus – He Who Resurrects." He then showed his hands and feet scarred with old wounds and his breast pierced by a spear. Said the man, "They slew me because of their independence and unbelief. So I have gone home to shut the doors of heaven that they may not see me again until the earth passes away."[6]

On another occasion, Grey Owl pointed out that Christianity initially had little impact on the Native American until they learned to read English. When that occurred and they read the first five books of Moses, many said, "Why, this is not the white man's religion; it is our old time belief."

In the book *He Walked the Americas* (Amherst Press, Amherst, Wisconsin, 1963), L. Taylor Hanson records numerous legends of the *Pale One,* who went among the Native Americans of North, Central and South America. The ancient Indians physically described this personage. His teachings were repeated to generations of Indians. In both the description and the teachings, it is obvious to see the outline of Jesus Christ in America; from the scars on his hands, to the color of his eyes; and from the healings he performed to the teachings he shared with them. Truly, Jesus' appearance in America is not one tribe's legend, or a fictional tale, the story of his appearance is written in the hearts and minds of many, many Native Americans.

Grey Owl, in his book, made one last plea to scholars concerning the origin of the Native American. He challenged them to reconsider their theories as to where and how the ancient people came to America. He emphatically states, "but there is one theory that is seldom approached except in jest...that is the persistent possibility that the Indians may be descendants of the House of Israel." As a minor substantiation of this comment, a stone was found in Tennessee in 1885 by a group of archeologists, known as the Bat Creek Stone. For years the scratching on the stone could not be deciphered, until the stone was turned right side up. Then the scratches became inscriptions and the language was recognized as Hebrew. The words? "For the land of Judah..."

This stone was only one of many reports of artifacts and inscriptions found throughout America that contained Hebrew letters or ancient Indian writings quoting Old Testament scriptures. My preference is not to recite all of these for you, but to point out that the evidence is mounting. Like the legends, the archeological discoveries here in America substantiate the existence of a people who knew about the land of Judea, the House of Israel, and even Jesus Christ.

Unlike the legends, the archeological discoveries are an independent, incorruptible, and tangible evidence of the existence of a Hebrew/Christian based society in America long before the arrival of Columbus. But the archeological discoveries cannot be viewed or understood in a vacuum. They are simply ancient, cold relics. The legends breathe life into them. The legends point the way of investigation and discovery, both in the physical and intellectual worlds (not to mention the spiritual world).

I don't want to leave you with the impression that only books by anthropologists, archeologists or Native Americans substantiate the message of this book. Each of their books is important in preserving the rich heritage of the Native American. But not found in books are the friendships and acquaintances I have had over the years with many wonderful and kind Native Americans. Some of whom I worked with and others who stayed in my home. One Indian friend named *Tecumseh Morgan,* whose father was a Cherokee Chief, told me about the *American Indian Exposition* that was held annually in Anadarko, Oklahoma. I traveled to the *Exposition* several times. Each time I met with many Native Americans and even had the opportunity to speak on the public address system that was heard throughout the camp. (Of course, I told them about the great things in store for them in the future.) Later, I took Tecumseh Morgan to a General Conference of The Church of Jesus Christ. Tecumseh believed the legends, but also accepted the Translated Ancient Nephite Record as the record of his people. He looked forward to the day when the Native Americans would unite and reclaim their place in America and before God.

A second friendship that I had was with *Chief Clinton Rickard,* of the Tuscarora Nation. Chief Rickard was instrumental in opening the border between Canada and the United States for Native Americans in the 1950's. I first met Chief Rickard at one of the crossing parades that the Indians held each year. In 1961, Chief Rickard and his son, William, spent time in my home. (As a side note, William was recognized for having developed new strains of corn.)

That same year, Chief Rickard invited me to attend the *Council of the Six Nations* that was held in Scranton, Pennsylvania. It was their first assembly in 200 years. I was given the opportunity to address the council and present the latter day message to those assembled regarding the great things God has in store for all Native Americans.

Chief Rickard was an ardent believer of the Translated Ancient Nephite Record. He knew it to be the record of his ancestors. He knew that his people were God's people and he also looked forward to the day when all Native Americans would have that knowledge and understanding and would unite together. (In the mid 1970's, I visited Mrs. Rickard in her home on the Tuscarora Reserve near Buffalo, New York. At that time, she re-affirmed her husband's beliefs.)

Finally, in the late 1970's, I made several visits to the *Seneca Nation of Indians* in Salamanca, New York with other dedicated ministers that I have been affiliated with for many years. Prior to one tribal meeting, we spent some time talking with Calvin Lay, who was the elected chief of the nation at that time. As we discussed the future of the Native American and the establishment of the Peaceful Reign and New Jerusalem in the land of America (see Chapter 13), he responded that our beliefs matched his. His beliefs foretold of the *New Society* that would be established one day by the Native Americans.

A few years back there was a bumper sticker that read, "Discover America, Read the Book of Mormon." To me there should be two bumper stickers. First, "Discover **Ancient** America, Read the Book of Mormon." And the second, "Discover America's **Future**, Read the Book of Mormon." You see, if the legends and archeological finds are correct in showing that there was a migration of Israelites to America in ancient times, then the Book of Mormon, which we have accepted by faith, **is** the record of those immigrants, and the word of God! And if the Book of Mormon is true, as we believe it to be, then not only is its history true, but its prophecies are true. And all people, Native Americans and Gentile Americans, must heed those prophecies, today!

Chapter 17

Jews and Native Americans – a Comparison

The seeds of this book were planted back in 1963 in a 35-page pamphlet that our grandfather called *Jew and American Indian.* Much of that pamphlet was incorporated into this book. The first edition of this book (1975) contained a chapter titled *Arabs and Israelites.* For the second edition (2002), this chapter was moved to an appendix and was updated. Although some things never seem to change (Middle East conflicts), some of the players in the conflict do change. The second edition warned that Sadam Hussain was trouble. He was, but is no more!

In reviewing the 2002 Appendix we felt that one area that our grandfather did not directly address in his pamphlet or the earlier editions of this book is the struggle that the Jews have endured for centuries in preserving their culture, language and land. For those who are Native Americans this struggle should sound familiar.

As his family, we are going to attempt to rectify that minor shortcoming, calling on our collective memories of Timothy, our father and grandfather, and his sermons, letters and articles. In particular, his relationship, not only with Native Americans, such as Tuscarora Chief Clinton Rickard, but with several Jewish Rabbis. So let's step back in time and review the struggle the Jews have endured.

Before we delve too deeply, we want to clear-up a misconception. Many today easily use the term Palestine and Palestinians (as found in this book). But to be more accurate, the land of Israel (in Hebrew, *Eretz Isra'el)* was not called Palestine until AD 135, some 1800 years after Abraham received the land from God. It was so named by the Roman Emperor Hadrian, who also assisted in the scattering of Jews throughout the Roman Empire.[7] During the ensuing years the land was occupied by Jews, Arabs, Egyptians, Turks, and others. All were called Palestinians. The situation is similar to all Native Americans being called Indians even though there were (and are) over 500 distinct nations, languages and cultures. It all changed in 1948 when the *State of Israel* was created (reborn) fulfilling many Biblical prophecies, as well as centuries of hopes, dreams and aspirations. Those who reside there are now called *Israelis.*

Where did the word Palestine come from? It was a derivative of ancient people called Philistines[8] (the Goliath of David and Goliath). These people were possibly Greeks who 3,000 years ago settled along the shores of what is now Gaza.[9] According to historians, the name Palestinian does not denote Arabs, but was applied to Jews before their state was formed. Zola Levitt (a Messianic Jew) noted that, "In fact, Arabs refused to be called Palestinians, because the Jews were known by that name. Arabs began to co-opt the term "Palestinian" after 1948 when the Jews renamed the country, and by 1964 when the PLO (Palestine Liberation Organization) was formed, it was completely taken over by the Arabs of the land." Mr. Levitt made the analogy that "there was no Palestinian culture in history, just as there was no Soviet [USSR] culture. The term "Soviet," which was applied to the various people who lived in Russia and its environs [satellite nations] for 70 years, has come and gone."[10]

Let us not forget who received the land from God – Abraham, Isaac, and Jacob (Genesis 12:1-3 and Deuteronomy 30:3-5). Any Arabs in the land are occupying Jewish land and not the other way around. Similarly, North, Central and South America were given to Jacob, who passed it on to his son Joseph,[11] the same Joseph who is the central figure of a number of chapters in this book and the forefather of most Native Americans.

An interesting fact not recognized by many people is that the Arabs in the State of Israel, who call themselves Palestinians, have mostly migrated to Israel since 1948. They were employed in construction and other skilled labor jobs, assisting in the building of a modern nation.

The modern concept of Zionism – the gathering of Jews to their God-given land – took hold in the mid to late nineteenth century[12] (interestingly, it was about 50 years after the publishing of the *Book of Mormon,* a sign that God was beginning to restore all of the promises to all of Israel). Jews living in Europe were experiencing both a renewed interest in their ancient land as well as anti-Semitic persecution. But it was not until 1882 when the first group of Jews immigrated to Israel (called Palestine at that time) to join those who had been living there for centuries. This movement was the *First Aliyah* (that is "going up" – as Jews describe their immigration to the

Holy Land).[13]

Between the early 1880s and the outbreak of the First World War in 1914, tens of thousands of Eastern European Jews immigrated to Israel.[14] While the flood of migrants to the region fell to a trickle during the war (1914-1918) the outcome of the conflict had an immediate impact on the future of Jews in the Near East. In an attempt to strengthen world-wide military and financial support for the Allies, British Foreign Secretary Arthur James Balfour issued the so-called *Balfour Declaration* on November 2, 1917. In the statement, Britain announced that they supported the establishment of a Jewish homeland in Palestine and would work toward the realization of that endeavor.[15]

At the time the region was controlled by the Ottoman Empire, a member of the Central Powers. Following Allied victory in 1918, the Ottoman Empire had much of her territories stripped and the Allied powers assumed administrative control of her former lands. The victorious powers were given "mandates" over certain areas whereby they would govern certain regions until such time as they were ready for independence. The British were granted control over the Mandate of Palestine and would administer the region according to the terms of the *Balfour Declaration*.[16] The area encompassed what are today the nations of Jordan and Israel, including the West Bank and Gaza. Between the end of World War I and the outbreak of World War II, hundreds of thousands of Jews migrated to Palestine. In 1918, the Jewish population had numbered only 58,000 out of a total of 800,000 people. By 1929 there were 170,000 Jews in Palestine and that number more than doubled to almost 500,000 by 1939.[17] Jewish settlers purchased large tracts of land and communities sprang up throughout the region. One of the first Jewish cities, Tel-Aviv, quickly grew to comprise approximately 60,000 people by 1933. Pioneers and investors began to develop the region agriculturally and economically as Jewish culture and industry began to thrive.[18] However, the rapidly expanding Jewish population led to rising political tensions with Palestinian Arabs. In the mid-1930s Arabs organized massive labor strikes that led to rioting and violence against Jews and British officials. In 1939, Britain began to severely restrict further Jewish immigration to Palestine and prohibited Jews from purchasing land outside of established Jewish settlements.[19]

During the Second World War which began in 1939, Nazi Germany targeted the Jewish population of Europe for extermination. In what became known as the "Final Solution," millions of Jews in regions under German occupation were rounded up and sent to death camps. By the time the war ended in 1945, between five to six million Jews had been systematically murdered. This number amounted to approximately one-quarter to one-third of the Jewish population of the entire world.[20]

As a result of Jewish suffering during World War II, the pressure to establish a homeland for Jews after centuries of struggle and discrimination finally became too much for the world community to ignore any longer. The United States led the way in pressuring the British government to permit the migration of displaced European Jews to Palestine. The newly established United Nations (UN) recommended that a Jewish state be established in Palestine and that the region should be divided between the Jews and the Arabs into two autonomous areas. In November 1947, the UN General Assembly approved the partition scheme. Unfortunately, Palestinian Arabs and the surrounding Arab nations condemned the decision.[21] Even before the war in Europe had ended, many Arab countries made it clear that they would do everything in their power to prevent the establishment of a Jewish state in Palestine. In October 1944 they organized the Arab League, which devoted itself to defending the rights of Arabs in Palestine. In early 1945, Saudi Arabia, Syria, Lebanon and Egypt warned that there would be dire consequences to any power that supported the establishment of a Jewish state in the Palestinian region.[22]

The warning proved prophetic. Within days of the UN's 1947 decision, attacks took place against Jews throughout the Muslim world and violence erupted in Palestine as the region descended into civil war. By the time the State of Israel was officially declared on May 14, 1948, the civil war turned into a general war as the Arab states of Egypt, Iraq, Jordan, Lebanon, Syria and Saudi Arabia declared war and invaded Israel.[23] Although the Israelis were outnumbered and outgunned, they fought with tenacity and not only succeeded in defending their territory, but actually capturing Arab lands. By the time the war ended in March 1949, the Israelis had secured their national independence and seized control of approximately 50% of the territory that had been allotted to the future Arab State of Palestine.[24]

An uneasy peace settled over the region, but tensions remained high between Israel and her Arab neighbors. The situation was especially tense between the new Jewish State and Egypt. From 1953-1955 the two sides engaged in a vicious border war that eventually escalated into a full scale war in 1956. Much of the tension revolved around the rise to power of Egyptian leader Gamal Abdel Nasser. Nasser was the leading proponent of pan-Arab nationalism, and hoped to unite the Arab world behind his leadership. He increased pressure on Israel by providing safe havens for Palestinians infiltrating Israel.[25] The final straw came in 1956 when Nasser nationalized the Suez Canal which had been under British control for decades. With the support of the French and the British, the Israelis launched an attack into the Sinai Peninsula. A few days later the French and British dispatched troops to seize and occupy the strategically important Suez Canal. While the operation was a military success, the world community and UN, including the United States, condemned the actions and Israel and the western powers were forced to withdraw their forces.[26]

In addition to international threats, Israel also faced conflict and violence at home. In 1964 the Palestinian Liberation Organization (PLO) was created. The group vowed to resist Zionism and declared that its goal was to liberate Palestine through armed struggle. A young PLO officer named Yasser Arafat formed the militant Fatah organization which adopted guerrilla warfare and terrorism in its fight against the Jewish state.[27]

As tensions with the PLO grew in the mid-1960s, Israel's neighbors also became more aggressive. In May 1967, Egyptian troops moved into the Sinai and approached the Israeli border. The Jordanians and Syrians also began to concentrate troops along their borders with Israel. Arab leaders made it clear that another war with Israel would be a war of annihilation in which the Jewish State would be wiped out.[28] Rather than wait for the inevitable attack, the Israeli's launched a pre-emptive strike against the surrounding Arab states of Egypt, Jordan and Syria on June 5, 1967. The so-called *Six Day War* was an overwhelming success for Israel. By the time the conflict ended on June 10, the Israelis had captured significant territory from their enemies. Israel now controlled the Sinai, the Golan Heights, the West Bank, Gaza and East Jerusalem. Many Israelis hoped that their resounding military victory would convince the Arab world that they would finally have to accept the Jewish state. Unfortunately, the Arab's response was just the opposite. The Arab League met and declared that there would be "no peace with Israel, no recognition of Israel and no negotiations with Israel."[29]

In 1970, Egyptian President Nasser died and was succeeded by Anwar Sadat. Sadat inherited a crumbling economy and a demoralized Egyptian population. Determined to push through a series of domestic reforms, Sadat desperately needed to first win the popular support of the people if his proposals were to stand any chance of success. The Egyptian leader saw a military strike against Israel and the reclamation of the Sinai as the means to achieve his objectives. On October 6, 1973, Egypt and Syria launched an attack and completely took Israel by surprise. The Israelis were preoccupied celebrating one of the holiest days in the Jewish calendar, **Yom Kippur,** or "Day of Atonement."[30] After some initial success in the Golan Heights and the Sinai, the Syrians and the Egyptians were finally repulsed, but not after the Egyptians had occupied a number of strategic points in the Sinai Peninsula. The United States, the Soviet Union and the UN all called for a ceasefire. Eventually, Egypt and Israel accepted the idea of undertaking direct negotiations that would lead to peace, an exchange of territory and recognition of the State of Israel.[31]

After a series of initial meetings between representative of Egypt and Israel, the leaders of the two countries finally met for face-to-face talks in the United States hosted by President Jimmy Carter. On September 17, 1978, Israel and Egypt signed the historic Camp David Accords. The agreement normalized relations between the two former adversaries and Egypt officially recognized the State of Israel, becoming the first Arab country to do so. Many Arab nations were unhappy with the agreement, especially the Palestinians who felt betrayed by Egypt.[32] Nevertheless, this historic treaty helped lay the groundwork for negotiations that would eventually bring a tentative peace deal between the Israelis and Palestinians in the early 1990s based upon the premise of a two state solution – an independent State of Palestine alongside of the State of Israel. [33]

A major step in this process occurred in September

1993 with the signing of the Oslo Accords between Israel and the PLO. With this settlement, the two sides agreed to officially recognize each other and vowed to put an end to hostilities between them. Although sporadic violence continued off and on, the peace process slowly moved forward. In accordance with the agreement, the Israelis gradually began to turn over control of the West Bank and Gaza to the Palestinian Authority, the name given to the newly organized Palestinian Arab government. In 2005, Israel officially pulled out of the Gaza Strip and completely turned the area over to the Palestinian Authority. However, following free elections in 2006, the radical Islamic group known as Hamas, assumed power in Gaza. Unlike the Palestinian Authority which governs Arab lands in the West Bank, Hamas has refused to recognize Israel and has committed itself to the destruction of the Jewish state.

So what do we conclude? We see that the Jews have struggled and continue to struggle for their independent state – a homeland. They have migrated from all over the world to their land of inheritance in the Middle East. In doing so, they have renewed the Hebrew language – long considered dead.

Native Americans struggle for recognition of their tribes, nations, languages, culture and customs, and for many a return of their homelands. Jews came from places in Europe called Ghettoes – or Jewish Quarters - areas in European towns in which the Jewish population was required to live. Similarly, Native Americans were removed from their lands of inheritance and forced onto reserves/reservations and into boarding schools.

The condition and situation of both Jews and Native Americans were prophesied in the *Book of Mormon,* which was published in 1830, many years prior to the Jewish Zionist Movement and before most of the removal and banishment of Native Americans by the federal governments of the Americas.

These prophecies, originally recorded between 600 BC and AD 400, speak of the restoration of the Jews after their scattering and abuse; that they would be gathered home to the lands of their inheritance; that after the federal governments camped against the Native Americans, laid siege to their villages, and erected forts against them, the prayers of the faithful shall be heard and the Native American (descendants of Joseph) shall not be forgotten by God, but instead he will

133

remember his covenant to them and raise them up as a great people. And at that time, the Native Americans (Joseph), the Jews (Judah), and the believing Gentiles will build a holy city unto the Lord God in America. And our Lord Jesus Christ will visit those who reside there. (See chapter 13.)

For those who would like to read the prophecies for themselves, here are a few examples.

And it came to pass that I, Nephi, spake much unto them concerning these things; yea, I spake unto them concerning the restoration of the Jews in the latter days. And I did rehearse unto them the words of Isaiah, who spake concerning the restoration of the Jews, or of the house of Israel; and after they were restored they should no more be confounded, neither should they be scattered again.

That he [God] has spoken unto the Jews, by the mouth of his holy prophets, even from the beginning down, from generation to generation, until the time comes that they shall be restored to the true church and fold of God [Messianic Jews]; when they shall be gathered home to the lands of their inheritance, and shall be established in all their lands of promise.

After my seed and the seed of my brethren [Native Americans] shall have dwindled in unbelief, and shall have been smitten by the Gentiles; yea, after the Lord God shall have camped against them round about, and shall have laid siege against them with a mount, and raised forts against them; and after they shall have been brought down low in the dust, even that they are not, yet the words of the righteous shall be written, and the prayers of the faithful shall be heard, and all those who have dwindled in unbelief shall not be forgotten.

O ye Gentiles, have ye remembered the Jews, mine ancient covenant people? Nay; but ye have cursed them, and have hated them, and have not sought to recover them [Anti-Semitism]. But behold, I will return all these things upon your own heads; for I the Lord have not forgotten my people.

And now, I would prophesy somewhat more concerning the Jews and the Gentiles. For after the book of which I have spoken shall come forth [the Book of Mormon], and be written unto the Gentiles, and sealed up again unto the Lord, there shall be many which shall believe the words which are written; and they shall carry them forth unto the remnant of our seed [Native Americans]. And then shall the remnant of our seed [Native Americans] know concerning us, how that we came out from Jerusalem, and that they are descendants of the Jews. And the gospel of Jesus Christ shall be declared among them; wherefore, they shall be restored unto the knowledge of their fathers, and also to the knowledge of Jesus Christ, which was had among their fathers. And then shall they rejoice; for they shall know that it is a blessing unto them from the hand of God; and their scales of darkness shall begin to fall from their eyes; and many generations shall not pass away among them, save they shall be a pure and delightsome people. And it shall come to pass that the Jews which are scattered also shall begin to believe in Christ; and they shall begin to gather in upon the face of the land; and as many as shall believe in Christ shall also become a delightsome people.

Yea, and ye need not any longer hiss, nor spurn, nor make game of the Jews, nor any of the remnant of the house of Israel; for behold, the Lord remembers his covenant unto them, and he will do unto them according to that which he hath sworn.

And behold, they shall go unto the unbelieving of the Jews [Book of Mormon]; and for this intent shall they go -- that they may be persuaded that Jesus is the Christ, the Son of the living God; that the Father may bring about, through his most Beloved, his great and eternal purpose, in restoring the Jews, or all the house of Israel, to the land of their inheritance, which the Lord their God hath given them, unto the fulfilling of his covenant.

Then shall ye, who are a remnant of the house of Jacob, go forth among them; and ye shall be in the midst of them who shall be many; and ye shall be among them as a lion among the beasts of the forest, and as a young lion among the flocks of sheep, who, if he goes through both treads down and tears in pieces, and none can deliver. Thy hand [Native Americans] shall be lifted up upon thine adversaries, and all thine enemies shall be cut off.

And when these things come to pass that thy seed [Native Americans] shall begin to know these things [Book of Mormon] -- it shall be a sign unto them, that they may know that the work of the Father hath already commenced unto the fulfilling of the covenant which he hath made unto the people who are of the house of Israel. And then shall the work of the Father commence at that day, even when this gospel shall be preached among the remnant of this people. Verily I say unto you, at that day shall the work of the Father commence among all the dispersed of my people [Native Americans and Jews], yea, even the tribes which have been lost, which the Father hath led away out of Jerusalem.

Chapter 18

World Concerns and the Future

I stated in the beginning of the book that the origin of the Israelites could be traced back about forty centuries to a man called Abraham, the father of the Jews or the Israelites. This very same man is also the father of the Arabs.

God made a covenant of grace with Abraham and in this covenant God promised Abraham that through his seed all nations, kindred, tongue, and people would be blessed (prophecy of the coming of Christ or Messiah). Also, a land would be given unto him and his posterity, a land flowing with milk and honey, for an everlasting possession. Here is the covenant that God made with Abraham as it is written in the Bible: "And I will establish my covenant between me and thee and thy seed after thee . . . the land wherein you are a stranger, all the land of Canaan, for an everlasting possession; and I will be their God." When God promised this land to Abraham (land of Canaan) it was in the possession of the Canaanites, who were descendants of Noah's grandson, Canaan. This land was also called the Promised Land, Palestine, and the Holy Land. The land of Canaan, which God promised Abraham and his posterity, was much larger than modern day Palestine.

After the deliverance of the Israelites from Egyptian bondage the Israelites were in the wilderness for forty years, led by Moses, the Deliverer. When Moses died, God chose another to lead the Israelites into the land of Canaan. His name was Joshua, and through his leadership the Israelites took over the land of Canaan as an everlasting possession as God had promised them. This land therefore, belongs to the Israelites. After the dispersion of the Jews throughout the world in AD 70, the gentiles controlled Palestine for many centuries. The Arabs entered Palestine and became what are known today as Palestinian Arabs. But to whom did God promise the land of Canaan? The Lord promised the land of Canaan to the seed of Abraham, Isaac, and Jacob (Israel) and his twelve sons, the nation of Israel. The Palestinian problem will not be solved until the nations of the world recognize God's covenant to Abraham, Isaac, and Jacob.

At the time God made this covenant, Abraham had no children. He and his wife were both very old, Abraham being about seventy and his wife about sixty. It was very difficult for them to believe that they would have children and that through their posterity a land would be given unto them and a Messiah would be born to bring salvation to all nations, kindred, tongue, and people. But God's word was fulfilled.

Believing that she could not bare children, Abraham's wife Sarah urged her husband to take Hagar, her Egyptian handmaid, so that he may obtain a child through her. Hagar conceived and gave birth to a son. An angel appeared to Hagar and informed her that the boy was to be called Ishmael.

After the birth of Ishmael, Sarah became jealous and despised Hagar. But the covenant that God made to Abraham was not to be through Ishmael. However, the Lord said concerning the descendants of Ishmael, that "...behold, I have blessed him, and will make him fruitful, and will multiply him exceedingly; twelve princes shall he beget, and I will make him a great nation." Thus Ishmael, the son of Hagar, became the father of the Arabs.

When Abraham was ninety-nine years old and Sarah eighty-nine, the Lord appeared unto him and said, "I am the Almighty God; walk before me, and be perfect. And I will make my covenant between me and thee, and will multiply thee exceedingly... As for me, behold, my covenant is with thee, and you shall be a father of many nations." Here the Lord renewed his covenant unto Abraham. But it was difficult for them to believe that Sarah could conceive and give birth at her age, for it was contrary to nature. But nothing is impossible with God, for He is a God of miracles, signs, and wonders.

Fourteen years after the birth of Ishmael, when Abraham was one hundred years old, and Sarah ninety, she gave birth to a son and he was called Isaac, "the seed of the promise." And through him and his son Jacob (Israel) came the Israelites, the house of Israel, or the twelve tribes of Israel.

Therefore, being descendants of Abraham, the Arabs and the Israelites are related to one another. The birth of Ishmael through Hagar and the birth of Isaac through Sarah, "the seed of the promise," brought friction between the two and their posterity. It is conceivable that much of the animosity and conflict between the Arabs and the Israelites can be traced back about 4,000 years.

The Middle East has been a problem for centuries. Since the dispersion of the Jews in AD 70 they have gone through much suffering and persecution, which apparently has fulfilled the prophecy concerning their situation in the world today. Throughout history the Jews have been victimized by enemies who have often vowed to destroy and exterminate them. And since Israel became a state on May 14, 1948 they have fought four wars to maintain their freedom and independence. Miraculously, they have been preserved. Why? Because it is the will of the Lord and because of the covenant that God made with Abraham, Isaac, and Jacob – a covenant of grace. God is true and his word shall not pass away. The Apostle Paul says, "For what if some did not believe? Shall their unbelief make the faith of God without effect? God forbid: yea, let God be true, but every man a liar; as it is written . . ."

The Scriptures teach that after the great tribulations, God will deal directly with the nations that fight against Israel and destroy them. Bible readers can see that many prophecies have been fulfilled and are being fulfilled even today. And so shall the prophecies of the future.

No nation or leaders of government that deny the existence of God as creator and His beloved Son Jesus can survive for any long period of time. Eventually, God will take a direct hand in punishing the wicked nations of the world. God has been merciful to the United States thus far. We have escaped the destruction, suffering and death of two World Wars and have been relatively free from great natural disasters and famine. But for how long? We, as a nation, have turned our backs to God.

Men are born to be free. The last surviving ancient American prophet between AD 400 and AD 421 warned this nation, saying, "...it is wisdom in God that these things be shown unto you, that thereby you may repent of your sins, and suffer not that these murderous combinations shall get above you, which are built up to get power and gain – and the work, yea, even the work of destruction come upon you, yea, even the sword of the justice of the Eternal God shall fall upon you, to your overthrow and destruction if ye shall suffer these things to be."

What do the prophets mean by "secret" and "murderous combinations" of which we read in the Translated Ancient Nephite Record? I am inclined to believe that it means gangs,

139

the Mafia (organized crime) and Muslim terrorists. It is no secret that they are out to destroy the freedoms of the world. As one of the prophets in the Translated Ancient Nephite Record states: Woe unto you if you allow this situation to prevail, for they seek "to overthrow the freedom of all lands, nations, and countries; and it brings to pass the destruction of all people, for it is built up by the devil, who is the father of all lies; even that same liar who beguiled our first parents, yea, even that same liar who has caused man to commit murder from the beginning; who has hardened the hearts of men that they have murdered the prophets, and stoned them, and cast them out from the beginning." Americans, let us turn to God and have faith in His beloved Son, repent and be baptized for the remission of sins and God will deliver his people.

All Americans (Jews, gentiles and American Indians) – come and seek the Lord. We need Him now more than ever in the history of the world. Since the coming forth of the Translated Ancient Nephite Record, the Lord has set His hand for the second time to restore His people to the land of their inheritance. The true gospel of Jesus Christ must be preached to all nations, kindred, tongue, and people. We are not only born to be free in the physical aspect, we are also born with a free mind, a free agent to choose right from wrong, righteous from evil, the kingdom of God or the kingdom of the devil. Which shall it be?

There are many religions in the world today. All differ in the concept of God or the Supreme Being. Some adherents are pagans and are idolatrous (idol worship). Others believe in monotheism (one God), while some are polytheistic (multiple or plurality of gods).

As there is a diversity of religions, there is also a division within the Christian faith. Diverse in faith and principles, there are many denominations that proclaim to teach the true doctrine of Christ. Unfortunately, many have apostatized from the New Testament church.

It is clear that many churches have failed in their responsibility to bring men unto God. How then can there be unity and peace among men? First, there is only one God. The Bible says, "The Lord our God, the Lord is one." There is also only one Christ. Therefore there should be one church of Christ, based upon the true points of his gospel. Even the name of the church should simply be called after him who gave his life for it.

An apostasy occurred in the Church and the Lord's authority was withdrawn, fulfilling Biblical prophecy. However, a restoration also occurred which restored the authority and brought out of the earth the Ancient Nephite Record. This record was then translated by the gift and power of God. The Apostasy lasted for about 1260 years, until the translation of the Ancient Nephite Record and its publication in 1830. Once again it gave man the authority to preach the true doctrine of Jesus Christ.

In the Translated Ancient Nephite Record we read of a young American prophet who predicted twenty-six hundred years ago that the American Indians would be smitten by the gentiles (Americans). However, the gentiles would be lifted up in pride and would stumble. And "because of the greatness of their stumbling block that they have built up many churches; nevertheless, they put down the power and miracles of God, and preach up unto themselves their own wisdom and their own learning, that they may get gain and grind upon the face of the poor." The young prophet stated:

And there are many churches built up which cause envy, and strife, and malice. And there are also secret combinations, [organized crime] even as in times of old, according to the combinations of the devil, [secret oaths] for he is the founder of all these things; yea, the founder of murder, and works of darkness; yea, and he leads them by the neck with a flaxen cord, until he binds them with his strong cords forever.

For behold, my beloved brethren, I say unto you that the Lord God works not in darkness. He does not anything save it be for the benefit of the world; for he loves the world, even that he lays down his own life that he may draw all men unto him. Wherefore, he commands none that they shall not partake of his salvation. Behold, does he cry unto any saying: Depart from me? Behold, I say unto you, Nay; but he says: 'Come unto me all ye ends of the earth, buy milk and honey, without money and without price.'

Behold, has he commanded any that they should depart out of the synagogues, or out of the houses of worship? Behold, I say unto you, Nay. Has he commanded any that they should not partake of his salvation? Behold I say unto you, Nay; but he has given it free for all men; and he has commanded his people that they should persuade all men to repentance.

Behold, has the Lord commanded any that they should not partake of his goodness? Behold I say unto you, Nay; but all men are privileged the one like unto the other, and none are forbidden. He commands that there shall be no priest crafts; for, behold, priest crafts are that men preach and set themselves up for a light unto the world, that they may get gain and praise of the world; but they seek not the welfare of Zion. Behold, the Lord has forbidden this thing; wherefore, the Lord God has given a commandment that all men should have charity, which charity is love. And except they should have charity they were nothing. Wherefore, if they should have charity they would not suffer the laborer in Zion to perish. But the laborer in Zion shall labor for Zion; for if they labor for money they shall perish.

And again, the Lord God has commanded that men should not murder; that they should not lie; that they should not steal; that they should not take the name of the Lord their God, in vain; that they should not envy; that they should not have malice; that they should not contend one with another; that they should not commit whoredoms; and that they should do none of these things; for who so does them shall perish.

For none of these iniquities come of the Lord; for he does that which is good among the children of men; and he does nothing save it be plain unto the children of men; and he invites them all to come unto him and partake of his goodness; and he denies none that come unto him, black and white, bond and free, male and female; and he remembers the heathen; and all are alike unto God, both Jew and Gentile.

The young prophet continued the prediction, saying:

But, behold, in the last days, or in the days of the Gentiles -- yea, behold all the nations of Gentiles and also the Jews, both those who shall come upon this land and those who shall be upon other lands, yea, even upon all the lands of the earth, behold, they will be drunken with iniquity and all manner of abominations. And when that day shall come they shall be visited of the Lord of Hosts, with thunder and with earthquake, and with a great noise, and with storm, and with tempest, and with the flame of devouring fire.

For it shall come to pass in that day that the churches which are built up, and not unto the Lord, when the one shall say

142

unto the other: Behold, I, I am the Lord's; and the others shall say: I, I am the Lord's; and thus shall everyone say that has built up churches, and not unto the Lord. And they shall contend one with another; and their priests shall contend one with another, and they shall teach with their learning, and deny the Holy Ghost, which gives utterance.

And they deny the power of God, the Holy One of Israel; and they say unto the people: Hearken unto us, and hear ye our precept; for behold there is no God today, [God is dead] for the Lord and the Redeemer has done his work, and he has given his power unto men; Behold, hearken ye unto my precept; if they shall say there is a miracle wrought by the hand of the Lord, believe it not; for this day he is not a God of miracles; he has done his work.

Yea, and there shall be many which shall say: Eat, drink, and be merry, for tomorrow we die; and it shall be well with us. And there shall also be many which shall say: Eat, drink, and be merry; nevertheless, fear God – he will justify in committing a little sin; yea, lie a little, take the advantage of one because of his words, dig a pit for thy neighbor; there is no harm in this; and do all these things, for tomorrow we die; and if it so be that we are guilty, God will beat us with a few stripes, and at last we shall be saved in the Kingdom of God.

Yea, and there shall be many which shall teach after this manner, false and vain and foolish doctrines and shall be puffed up in their hearts, and shall seek deep to hide their counsels from the Lord; and their works shall be in the dark. Because of pride, and because of false teachers, and false doctrine, their churches have become corrupted, and their churches are lifted up; because of pride they are puffed up. They rob the poor because of their fine sanctuaries; they rob the poor because of their fine clothing; and they persecute the meek and the poor in heart, because in their pride they are puffed up.

They wear stiff necks and high heads; yea, and because of pride, and wickedness, and abominations, and whoredoms, they have all gone astray save it be a few, who are the humble followers of Christ; nevertheless, they are led, that in many instances they do err because they are taught by the precepts of men.

O the wise, and the learned, and the rich, that are puffed up in the pride of their hearts, and all those who preach false doctrines, and all those who commit whoredoms, and pervert the right way of the Lord, wo, wo, wo be unto them, says the Lord God Almighty, for they shall be thrust down to hell! Woe unto them that turn aside the just for a thing of naught and revile against that which is good, and say that is of no worth! For the day shall come that the Lord God will speedily visit the inhabitants of the earth; and in that day that they are fully ripe in iniquity they shall perish. But behold, if the inhabitants of the earth shall repent of their wickedness and abominations they shall not be destroyed, says the Lord of Hosts.

And behold, others he flatters away, and tells them there is no hell; and he says unto them: I am no devil, for there is none – and thus he whispers in their ears, until he grasps them with his awful chains, from whence there is no deliverance. Yea, they are grasped with death, and hell; and death, and hell, and the devil, and all that have been seized wherewith must stand before the throne of God, and be judged according to their works, from whence they must go into the place prepared for them, even a lake of fire and brimstone, which is endless torment.

This young Israelite prophet had predicted this about 2500 years ago through a revelation from God. He was taken up in the spirit to a high mountain and saw the world as it exists today. He was commanded to write on gold plates that were eventually translated by a farm boy (Joseph Smith Jr.) through the gift and power of God. The Translated Ancient Nephite Record has many prophecies and many of these have already been fulfilled.

It is apparent that American society in the last decade has deteriorated. Crime, drug abuse, pornography, destruction of public and private property and violence are at their worst. How long will God tolerate these conditions? Our nation has become immoral. Men of high position have betrayed our country. Honesty and integrity are talked about, but not adhered to. When a fruit becomes ripe it falls, so it is with the iniquities of a nation. Such a nation cannot stand. Our freedom, democracy and way of life depend on the spiritual life of the country. This nation of ours is the greatest nation in the entire world. God has blessed this land above all other lands. We must remember to love the true living God, our country and our fellow man.

After the great tribulations and sufferings in the Americas, God is going to take a direct hand in setting up the Western Hemisphere as a place of happiness and peace for those who are righteous and holy. The Lord will destroy the wicked and spare the righteous. A holy city, which shall be called the New Jerusalem, will be established in America and there will be a reign of peace in the Americas that will last for a long time. This is often referred to as *Zion,* the *Peaceful Reign,* or the *First Dominion.* The prophet Isaiah gives a wonderful description of this peaceful reign. An infant shall be a hundred years old and old men shall be hundreds of years old. Listen to this prophecy:

> And they shall build houses, and inhabit them; and they shall plant vineyards, and eat the fruit of them. They shall not build, and another inhabit; they shall not plant, and another eat: for as the days of a tree are the days of my people, and mine elect shall long enjoy the work of their hands. They shall not labor in vain, nor bring forth for trouble; for they are the seed of the blessed of the Lord, and their offspring with them. And it shall come to pass, that before they call, I will answer; and while they are yet speaking, I will hear. The wolf and the lamb shall feed together, and the lion shall eat straw like the bullock: and dust shall be the serpent's meat. They shall not hurt nor destroy in all my holy mountain, says the Lord.

This will be the new America of tomorrow established by the Lord for those who are righteous and holy. American Indians, Jews, and all the American people – great things await you if you would only turn to the God of Abraham, Isaac, and Jacob, the God of the Jewish prophets and Apostles, and also the God of the ancient American prophets and the disciples. Come! Ask this great God and creator of all things with faith in the Lord Jesus Christ and it shall be revealed to you by the power of the Holy Ghost that these things are true. For it is by the Holy Ghost that ye shall know the truth of all things.

The American Indian Moses is a descendant of Joseph, the son of Jacob (Israel), who was the great-grandson of Abraham. He will be a principal person in bringing about the establishment of Zion in America.

The headquarters of The Church of Jesus Christ will be here in America. The Prophet Micah certainly implies this when he says:

But in the last days it shall come to pass, that the mountain of the house of the Lord shall be established in the top of the mountains, and it shall be exalted above the hills; and people shall flow unto it. And many nations shall come, and say, Come, and let us go up to the mountain of the Lord, and to the house of the God of Jacob; and he will teach us of his ways, and we will walk in his paths: for the law shall go forth of Zion, [America] and the word of the Lord from Jerusalem.

And he shall judge among many people, and rebuke strong nations afar off; and they shall beat their swords into plowshares, and their spears into pruning hooks: nation shall not lift up a sword against nation, neither shall they learn war any more. But they shall sit every man under his vine and under his fig tree; and none shall make them afraid: for the mouth of the Lord of hosts has spoken it.

This *Peaceful Reign,* or *Zion in America,* will exist for a long time. It will be a period of blood life (before the resurrection). People shall labor and enjoy the fruits of their labor. They shall marry and be given in marriage. There shall be no contentions, and no evil, because of the great love for the Lord and for one another. The Lord Jesus Christ will appear and be in their midst from time to time. The blessings of God will be tremendous. During the Peaceful Reign in America there shall be great distress, trials, and tribulations among the nations of the world as they battle against the nation of Israel. There will be great suffering in Israel. However, the Lord will take a direct hand in the matter and deliver His people, and they shall finally come to the knowledge of the Messiah as their Redeemer.

The headquarters of the church in America will send out servants of the Lord for the last time (Government of God) in the vineyard (earth) to gather His people, the House of Israel. These servants of the Lord shall go forth in power to bring about the restoration of the House of Israel to the land of their inheritance. How blessed are they who have labored diligently in His vineyard. After these things, the world shall be burned with fire, the wicked destroyed, and the righteous saved. The earth shall be made a paradise for the abiding of the **resurrected** people of God. Christ shall dwell with them for a thousand years – this is the first resurrection referred to by Apostle John. After the thousand years, Satan will be loosed from prison, and shall go out to deceive the nations of the world. "Blessed and holy is he that has part in the first resurrection: on such the second death has no power . . ."

As I stated earlier, the American Indians are from the house of Israel, descendants of Joseph who was carried captive into Egypt, and great were the covenants of the Lord that He made unto Joseph. Thus the term SEED OF JOSEPH is sometimes used when referring to the American Indians. As God selected Moses to be a DELIVERER unto the House of Israel He is going to call out of the American Indian nation someone similar to Moses, a DELIVERER or CHOICE SEER, to bring about the restoration of the Seed of Joseph to the land of their inheritance (America). And through him and the servants of the Lord, "the Messiah should be made manifest unto them in the latter days, in spirit and power, unto the bringing of them out of darkness unto light – yea, out of hidden darkness and out of captivity unto freedom." The Indian Moses is going to be of great worth to them and they shall esteem him highly and the Lord will make him great in His eyes even to bring them knowledge of the covenants the Lord made to the House of Israel. God will give him a commandment that he shall do no other work except what God shall command him. The Lord will make a spokesman for him and He shall bring the word to his people with great power. He will be blessed and some will seek to destroy him, but they shall be confounded.

This **American Indian Moses** will be instrumental in the hands of God. A man of exceeding faith, he will work mighty wonders and help restore the American Indians to the House of Israel. The Lord has already set His hand for the second time, since the Ancient Nephite Records have been translated. Prophecies of the Bible and the Translated Ancient Nephite Records are being fulfilled at this very moment. The time is approaching when God will take a direct hand in the affairs of the nations of the world. Then He will speedily bring to a climax the great events that are to transpire in the world in these last days.

The prophecy of the Apostle Paul in his second letter to Timothy chapter three describes the situation in the world today: "This know also, that in the last days perilous times shall come. For men shall be lovers of their own selves, covetous, boasters, proud, blasphemers, disobedient to parents, unthankful, unholy, Without natural affection, trucebreakers, false accusers, incontinent fierce, despisers of those that are good, Traitors, heady, high-minded, lovers of pleasures more than lovers of God; Having a form of godliness, but denying the power thereof: from such turn away." Isn't it incredible how God clearly revealed the situation in the world today to the Apostle Paul?   Oh how great and marvelous are thy works, Lord God Almighty! Thy throne is high in the heavens, and thy power, and goodness, and mercy is over all the inhabitants of the earth, because you are merciful, you will not suffer those who come unto thee that they shall perish!

As Paul puts it – "Lovers of pleasures more than lovers of God" – is precisely true.   The majority of the people today seek physical instead of spiritual pleasure.   For most, concerts, sporting events and other forms of entertainment are more important than their personal relationship with the Lord and His Gospel.   Despite the fact that the world is waxing worse and that Jesus said, "And because iniquity shall abound, the love of many shall wax cold," there are still many fine people in the world. Many of them though are led astray because of the precepts and commandments of men. However, God is going to raise up a people, the Saints of the most high God to dwell on the earth. The New Jerusalem will be established in America, and in Palestine the Old Jerusalem will once again become a holy, righteous and eternal city.

A prophet in the first part of the fifth century AD prophesied concerning the gentiles in these last days, warning those who spurn the words and works of the Lord, saying:

And now behold, I say unto you that when the Lord shall see fit, in his wisdom, that these sayings shall come unto the Gentiles [Americans] according to his word, then ye may know that the covenant which the Father has made with the children of Israel, concerning their restoration to the lands of their inheritance, is already beginning to be fulfilled. And ye may know that the words of the Lord, which have been spoken by the holy prophets, shall all be fulfilled; and ye need not say that the Lord delays his coming unto the children of Israel. And ye need not imagine in your hearts that the words which have been spoken are vain, for behold, the Lord will remember his covenant which he has made unto his people of the house of Israel. And when ye shall see these sayings coming forth among you, then ye need not any longer spurn at the doings of the Lord, for the sword of his justice is in his right hand; and behold, at that day, if ye shall spurn at his doings he will cause that it shall soon overtake you. Wo unto him that spurns at the doings of the Lord; yea, wo unto him that shall deny the Christ and his works! Yea, wo unto him that shall deny the revelations of the Lord, and that shall say the Lord no longer works by revelation, or by prophecy, or by gifts, or by tongues, or by healing, or by the power of the Holy Ghost!

Yea, and wo unto him that shall say at that day, to get gain, that there can be no miracle wrought by Jesus Christ; for he that does this shall become like unto the son of perdition, for whom there was no mercy, according to the word of Christ! Yea, and ye need not any longer hiss, nor spurn, nor make game of the Jews, nor any of the remnant of the house of Israel [American Indians]; for behold, the Lord remembers his covenant unto them, and he will do unto them according to that which he has sworn. Therefore ye need not suppose that ye can turn the right hand of the Lord unto the left, that he may not execute judgment unto the fulfilling of the covenant which he has made unto the house of Israel.

This very same American prophet calls the inhabitants of the earth, especially the Americans, to repentance, saying:

Hearken, 0 ye Gentiles, and hear the words of Jesus Christ, the Son of the living God, which he has commanded me that I should speak concerning you, for, behold he commands me that I should write saying: Turn, all ye Gentiles, from your wicked ways; and repent of your evil doing, of your lying and deceiving, and of your whoredom, and of your secret abominations, and your idolatries, and of your murders, and your priest crafts, and your envying, and your strife, and from all your wickedness and abominations, and come unto me, and be baptized in my name, that ye may receive a remission of sins, and be filled with the Holy Ghost, that ye may be numbered with my people who are of the house of Israel.

Jews, Gentiles, and American Indians, let me reassert the words of the last surviving American prophet from about AD 421. These were the last writings inscribed in the Ancient Nephite Records before they were buried in the earth. They remained there for fourteen hundred years until Joseph Smith Jr. was shown them, and given permission by the messenger of God to take and translate them by the gift and the power of God:

And I seal up these records, after I have spoken a few words by way of exhortation unto you. Behold, I would exhort you that when ye shall read these things, if it be wisdom in God that ye should read them, that ye would remember how merciful the Lord has been unto the children of men, from the creation of Adam even down until the time that ye shall receive these things, and ponder it in your hearts. And when ye shall receive these things, I would exhort you that ye would ask God, the Eternal Father, in the name of Christ, if these things are not true; and if ye shall ask with a sincere heart, with real intent, having faith in Christ, he will manifest the truth of it unto you, by the power of the Holy Ghost. And by the power of the Holy Ghost, ye may know the truth of all things. And whatsoever thing is good is just and true; wherefore, nothing that is good denies the Christ, but acknowledges that he is. And ye may know that he is, by the power of the Holy Ghost; wherefore I would exhort you that ye deny not the power of God; for he works by power, according to the faith of the children of men, the same today and tomorrow, and forever.

And again, I exhort you, my brethren that ye deny not the gifts of God, for they are many; and they come from the same God. And there are different ways that these gifts are administered; but it is the same God who works all in all; and they are given by the manifestations of the spirit of God unto men, to profit them.

In conclusion, may I, the author of this book, say when my physical life comes to an end, my faith and hope are that I will go to rest in the Paradise of God until my spirit and body shall reunite and emerge triumphant through the air to meet my Lord and Savior Jesus Christ, and dwell with Him for a thousand years upon the earth. After the thousand years, I shall be with Christ and my God for eternity. **Amen.**

Epilogue

Timothy's physical life came to an end on April 23, 1997; but his work lives on. He was a man of faith in Christ Jesus and a man of prayer and good works. We who are left behind can say he lived as he believed; he died as he lived. He leaves for us a legacy and, more importantly, a vision. Much of that vision is contained in this book. We hope you, too, will see it, feel it, understand it, and be moved to share it just as he was.

Lineage Tree of Abraham, Jesus and the Choice Seer

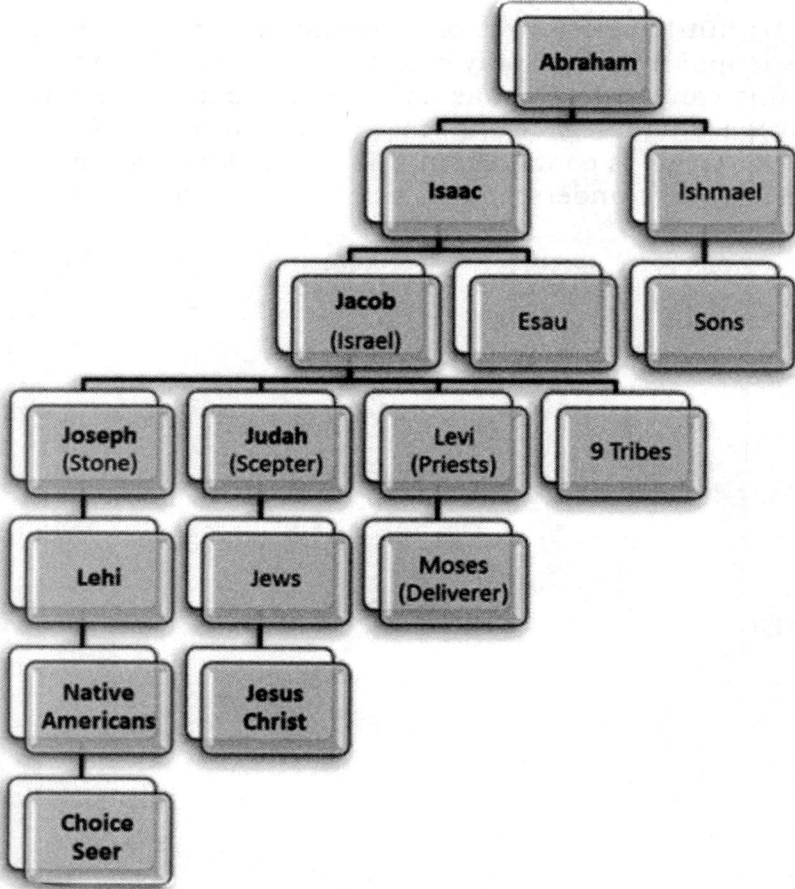

Scriptural Timeline

(All dates are approximates to provide some comparison and are based on Biblical/historical scholars)

YEAR	EVENT	LOCATION
4000 BC	Adam and Eve sin against God	Garden of Eden
2300 BC	Noah and the Flood	Mt. Ararat
2200 BC	Tower of Babel; God leads Brother of Jared and families (Jaredites) to a new land	Plains of Shinar to America
1950 BC	Abram (later Abraham) is born	Ur of the Chaldeans
1865 BC	Isaac is born in Canaan to Abraham and Sarah	Land of Canaan
1805 BC	Jacob and Esau are born to Isaac and Rebekah	Land of Canaan
1915 BC	Joseph, son of Jacob and Rachel, is born	Land of Canaan
1900 BC	Joseph sold as a slave by his jealous brothers and is taken to Egypt	Land of Canaan
1875 BC	Jacob and eleven sons and families relocate due to famine	Egypt
1445 BC	Moses is selected by God to be Israel's deliverer	Horeb in Midian
1405 BC	After wandering in the wilderness for forty years with Moses, Joshua is selected by God to lead Israel into Canaan, destroying the idolatrous Canaanites	Wilderness and then Canaan
1200 BC	Israel is ruled by "Judges"	Israel
1045 BC	Israelites demand a king; God selects Saul as king of Israel	Israel
1005 BC	David becomes king and makes Jerusalem his capital	Israel
970 BC	David's son Solomon becomes king and builds first temple	Jerusalem
930 BC	Solomon dies and kingdom is split – Northern Kingdom of Israel and Southern Kingdom of Judah and Benjamin	Israel
722 BC	Capital of Israel, Samaria, is conquered by the Assyrians, who scatter ten tribes into the north country	Israel

YEAR	EVENT	LOCATION
600 BC	Prophet Lehi is instructed by God to flee and is directed to a promised land (Ancient America)	Jerusalem to Ancient America
590 BC	Mulek, only remaining son of King Zedekiah of Judah, is taken to America	Land of Zarahemla in Ancient America
586 BC	Jerusalem is destroyed and many Jews carried off to Babylon	Jerusalem
580 BC	Mulekites in America find last surviving Jaredite from Babel colony	Zarahemla
515 BC	Second temple is built and dedicated by Jews returning from Babylonia captivity	Jerusalem
180 BC	Nephites discover Mulekites (now called people of Zarahemla)	Zarahemla
91 BC	Nephites change government from monarchy to democracy with "judges"	Zarahemla
44 BC	Roman Republic ends and Empire begins with death of Julius Caesar; conquered land of Judea is given to King Herod	Southern Europe and Middle East
*****	Prophesied signs of Jesus' birth occur; wise men from the east come to Jerusalem following a new star	Ancient America and Jerusalem
34 to 200 AD	Church of Jesus Christ established in Judea and America; complete peace in the land of America – greatly blessed of God; Church in Jerusalem grows quickly and spreads throughout the region	America and Middle East
70 AD	Romans destroy temple and Jerusalem	Jerusalem
400-500 AD	Apostasy of Church as prophesied – its doctrines and ordinances corrupted and authority taken away by God	America and then Europe and Middle East
1827 AD	Joseph Smith Jr. receives Ancient American Indian Record (on plates of gold) and translates it into English by gift and power of God through ancient interpreters	Palmyra, New York
1829 – 1830 AD	Church of Jesus Christ is established again with spiritual gifts, power and authority of God	New York
1844 AD	Joseph Smith is murdered	Carthage, Illinois

Year	Event	Location
1862 AD	The Church of Jesus Christ is organized with William Bickerton as Apostle and President	Greenock, PA (now Monongahela, PA)
1870's to present	Missionary outreach among Native Americans	Indian Territory; reserves and reservations; and urban centers
Future	Choice Seer (promised *American Indian Moses*) performs work God has commanded him to do	Americas
Future	Stone Kingdom, First Dominion (also called Peaceful Reign) begins (see Isaiah 2 and 11 and Daniel 2)	Americas
Future	New Jerusalem is built by descendants of Jacob and Joseph, and righteous people are gathered into it	America

Index

End Notes

[1] Isaiah 10:21; 35:10; Jeremiah 12:15; 31:8; 2 Nephi 10:7; 25:11; 3 Nephi 16:5; 20:22

[2] US Census for 2010

[3] I am not suggesting that Columbus was a righteous man but that God used him for God's purposes, such as the Persian king, Cyrus; see 2 Chronicles 36:22

[4] 2 Kings 19:30-31 and Ezekiel 17:22-24

[5] Daniel 2:44, 45

[6] http://www.sacred-texts.com/nam/iro/parker/index.htm

[7] en.wikipedia/wiki/History_of_Palestine

[8] www.Leavitt.com/essays/palestine.html

[9] Answers.Yahoo.com/question/index?qid=20110313151446Aancw7k

[10] www.Leavitt.com/newsletters/2000-12

[11] Genesis 49:26; Deuteronomy 33:13-17

[12] www.Leavitt.com/essays/dh.html

[13] www.jewishhistory.org/the-first-aliyah/

[14] See Gur Alroey, *An Unpromising Land: Jewish Migration to Palestine in the Early Twentieth Century* (Stanford, CA: Stanford University Press, 2014).

[15] Cecil Roth, *A History of the Jews: From Earliest Times Through the Six Day War, (New York: Schocken Books, 1970),* 364-374.

[16] Roth, 374.

[17] Peter L. Hahn, *Caught in the Middle East: U.S. Policy toward the Arab-Israeli Conflict, 1945-1961,* (Chapel Hill, NC: The University of North Carolina Press, 2004), 13; Roth, 375, 386.

[18] Roth, 376.

[19] Hahn, 13-14; Roth, 386-388.

[20] Roth, 408.

[21] Roth, 412-414.

[22] Hahn, 14.

[23] Roth, 414-418.

[24] Hahn, 62; Roth, 417-420.

[25] Hahn, 163; Roth 423.

[26] Hahn, 200-209; Roth 423-424.

[27] Stephen P. Cohen, *Beyond America's Grasp: A Century of Failed Diplomacy in the Middle East,* (New York: Farrar, Straus and Giroux, 2009), 203.

[28] Cohen, 204; Roth, 433.

[29] Cohen, 204-206; Roth, 434-436.

[30] Day of Atonement – Leviticus 23:27-28.

[31] Cohen, 209-211.

[32] Cohen, 213-224.

[33] Isaiah 19: 19-25

Why We Believe What We Believe and Why it Matters to You

The Grandchildren of Timothy Dom Bucci

In the pages of this book our grandfather refers to a spiritual/historical record he affectionately called the Translated Ancient American Indian Record. Its more common names are Nephite Record and Book of Mormon. One of the reasons he wrote the book was to explain how important this book is for you.

As he showed, the Book of Mormon is similar to the Bible in that it is a holy, spiritual, and civil record of the ancient Israelite people. Although the time period it covers is shorter, it is focused on a people God brought to ancient America from the land of Jerusalem and how he dealt with them and how they dealt with each other. It is about their prophets and their rulers, their blessings and their struggles.

This book contains many beautiful teachings, prophecies, and accounts of holy men of God who were the forefathers of modern day Native Americans. So in reality, the Book of Mormon is a book that belongs to the Native American – it is your book. It just so happened that God used a non-Native to translate the book from its ancient language to English and He asked a non-Indian people (us) to carry it back to Native Americans for them to see what great things God did for their forefathers and to complete His plan for all of Israel.

You may ask what you should do with the book. First, notice that the book establishes God's selection of Israel as his covenant people (including Native Americans) and that He will gather them together one day soon. It also testifies that Jesus Christ is the only begotten son of God, the Savior and Redeemer of the world. And it prophesies that a spiritual renewal and awakening will occur in the Americas led by Native Americans. In many respects, the book is the true culture of the Native American.

So you may now ask, why are we explaining all of this to you? Because we want to do our part in carrying out the will of God, i.e. returning your ancient and holy record back to you as we were told to do by God. You see, we are only messengers of God, carrying out His plans that he foretold, in the Bible, thousands of years ago. We are similar to John the Baptist, who fulfilled the prophecy of the coming of Jesus by the Prophet Isaiah (Isaiah 40:3).

There is an old saying, "The truth may be hard to bear, but it stands on its own." We want to show you how beautiful and inspiring this ancient record is, so here are a few quotes from it. See if they do not touch your heart, connect with your spirit, and inspire your mind.

I will go and do the things which the Lord hath commanded, for I know that the Lord gives no commandments unto the children of men, save he shall prepare a way for them that they may accomplish the thing which he commands them. (1 Nephi 3:7)

Wherefore, how great the importance to make these things known unto the inhabitants of the earth, that they may know that there is no flesh that can dwell in the presence of God, save it be through the merits, and mercy, and grace of the Holy Messiah, who lays down his life according to the flesh, and takes it again by the power of the Spirit, that he may bring to pass the resurrection of the dead, being the first that should rise. (2 Nephi 2:8)

But behold, all things have been done in the wisdom of him who knows all things. (2 Nephi 2:24)

O, remember, my son, and learn wisdom in thy youth; yea, learn in thy youth to keep the commandments of God. Yea, and cry unto God for all thy support; yea, let all thy doings be unto the Lord, and whithersoever you go let it be in the Lord; yea, let all thy thoughts be directed unto the Lord; yea, let the affections of thy heart be placed upon the Lord forever. Counsel with the Lord in all thy doings, and he will direct thee for good; yea, when you lie down at night lie down unto the Lord, that he may watch over you in your sleep; and when you rise in the morning let thy heart be full of thanks unto God; and if ye do these things, ye shall be lifted up at the last day. (Alma 37:35-37)

And behold, I tell you these things that ye may learn wisdom; that ye may learn that when ye are in the service of your fellow beings ye are only in the service of your God. (Mosiah 2:17)

But behold, I say unto you that ye must pray always, and not faint; that ye must not perform anything unto the Lord save in the first place ye shall pray unto the Father in the name of Christ, that he will consecrate thy performance unto thee, that thy performance may be for the welfare of thy soul. (2 Nephi 32:9)

Yea, Joseph truly said: Thus saith the Lord unto me: A choice seer will I raise up out of the fruit of thy loins [descendants]; and he shall be esteemed highly among the fruit of thy loins [Native Americans]. And unto him will I give commandment that he shall do a work for the fruit of thy loins, his brethren, which shall be of great worth unto them, even to the bringing of them to the knowledge of the covenants which I have made with thy fathers. (2 Nephi 3:7)

Are ye willing to mourn with those that mourn; yea, and comfort those that stand in need of comfort, and to stand as witnesses of God at all times and in all things, and in all places that ye may be in, even until death, that ye may be redeemed of God, and numbered with those of the first resurrection, that ye may have eternal life... (Mosiah 18:9)

And if men come unto me I will show unto them their weakness. I give unto men weakness that they may be humble; and my grace is sufficient for all men that humble themselves before me; for if they humble themselves before me, and have faith in me, then will I make weak things become strong unto them. Behold, I will show unto the Gentiles their weakness, and I will show unto them that faith, hope and charity brings unto me—the fountain of all righteousness. (Ether 12: 27:28)

And now, I, Moroni, would speak somewhat concerning these things; I would show unto the world that faith is things which are hoped for and not seen; wherefore, dispute not because ye see not, for ye receive no witness until after the trial of your faith. (Ether 12:6)

For the fullness of mine intent is that I may persuade men to come unto the God of Abraham, and the God of Isaac, and the God of Jacob, and be saved. (1 Nephi 6:4)

And now, my beloved son, notwithstanding their hardness, let us labor diligently; for if we should cease to labor, we should be brought under condemnation; for we have a labor to perform whilst in this tabernacle of clay, that we may conquer the enemy of all righteousness, and rest our souls in the kingdom of God. (Moroni 9:6)

Yea, come unto Christ, and be perfected in him, and deny yourselves of all ungodliness; and if ye shall deny yourselves of all ungodliness and love God with all your might, mind and strength, then is his grace sufficient for you, that by his grace ye may be perfect in Christ; and if by the grace of God ye are perfect in Christ, ye can in nowise deny the power of God.(Moroni 10:32)

Behold, it came to pass that I, Enos, knowing my father that he was a just man -- for he taught me in his language, and also in the nurture and admonition of the Lord -- and blessed be the name of my God for it And I will tell you of the wrestle which I had before God, before I received a remission of my sins. Behold, I went to hunt beasts in the forests; and the words which I had often heard my father speak concerning eternal life, and the joy of the saints, sunk deep into my heart. And my soul hungered; and I kneeled down before my Maker, and I cried unto him in mighty prayer and supplication for mine own soul; and all the day long did I cry unto him; yea, and when the night came I did still raise my voice high that it reached the heavens. And there came a voice unto me, saying: Enos, thy sins are forgiven thee, and thou shalt be blessed. And I, Enos, knew that God could not lie; wherefore, my guilt was swept away. And I said: Lord, how is it done? And he said unto me: Because of thy faith in Christ, whom thou hast never before heard nor seen. And many years pass away before he shall manifest himself in the flesh; wherefore, go to, thy faith hath made thee whole.(Enos 1:1-8)

Adam fell that men might be; and men are, that they might have joy. (2 Nephi 2:25)

And they [Gentiles] shall assist my people, the remnant of Jacob, and also as many of the house of Israel as shall come, that they may build a city, which shall be called the New Jerusalem. And then shall they assist my people that they may be gathered in, who are scattered upon all the face of the land, in unto the New Jerusalem. And then shall the power of heaven come down among them; and I also will be in the midst. (3 Nephi 21:23-25)

And now, my sons, remember, remember that it is upon the rock of our Redeemer, who is Christ, the Son of God, that ye must build your foundation; that when the devil shall send forth his mighty winds, yea, his shafts in the whirlwind, yea, when all his hail and his mighty storm shall beat upon you, it shall have no power over you to drag you down to the gulf of misery and endless wo, because of the rock upon which ye are built, which is a sure foundation, a foundation whereon if men build they cannot fall. (Helaman 5:12)